Praise for *Amplify* You

Gina London brings her formidable talents to the task of helping us communicate better. Now more than ever, we need a book that shows us why communication is so vital to human connection and exactly how we can get better at it. Gina does exactly that, with warmth, wisdom and actionable tools.

—Dr. Robert Waldinger

Professor of Psychiatry, Harvard Medical School and Director, Harvard Study of Adult Development, Zen Master and New York Times *bestselling author of* The Good Life

If you want to communicate with greater confidence, clarity, and impact, *Amplify You* is your guide. Drawing from her experience coaching top executives worldwide, Gina London offers actionable strategies to help leaders inspire, connect, and lead with purpose. Engaging and insightful, this book is a must-read for anyone striving to elevate their influence and master the language of leadership.

—Liz Wiseman

New York Times *bestselling author of* Multipliers *and* Impact Players

To be heard and seen, you need to amplify yourself. That doesn't mean getting louder. It means getting clearer and more confident. This book will help you with both.

—Michael Bungay Stanier

Author of the million-copy Wall Street Journal *bestseller* The Coaching Habit

The first time I met Gina London, I felt an instant connection—like I had known her for years, even though we had just met. As both a speaker and an audience member at a memorable event she was hosting, I was immediately drawn in by her warmth, authenticity, and effortless ability to engage. That ease of communication is part natural gift, part hard-won, experience-driven wisdom.

That's why I'm so thrilled that, in her new book, *Amplify You*, Gina is sharing these gifts with the world. Her insights are powerful, practical, and deeply inspiring. Read it—you won't regret it!

—Dr. Wendy Suzuki

Dean of the College of Arts and Science and Professor of Neural Science and Psychology, New York University. New York Times *bestselling author of* Healthy Brain, Happy Life *and* Good Anxiety

When Gina London asked to interview me for her column in Ireland's *Sunday Independent* newspaper, I wasn't sure what to expect. I saw her history as a CNN reporter and her major clients in different countries and it made me wonder just how she would show up.

When we met in Dublin, what I found was within minutes I was naturally sharing and discussing issues. She made it so easy to be open. Her genuine interest in my work made it seem like we had been friends for some time. She was the epitome of what she teaches about communication.

In *Amplify You*, Gina provides the skills and mindsets that help you confidently bring your genuine self to whatever you are doing.

—Dave Jennings

Wall Street Journal *bestselling author of* The Pit of Success

Elevate your communication, refine your presence, and amplify your impact with *Amplify You*. Gina London's expert insights and interactive tools make connecting with confidence and clarity easy. If you're ready to communicate like never before, then start reading right now.

—Rhett Power

Forbes *columnist and CEO of Accountability Inc.*

In a world where AI is rapidly transforming how we work and interact, Gina London reminds us that the most powerful tool we have is still our own humanity. *Amplify You* is a masterclass in purposeful connection—helping you take charge of your voice, body language, and behavior to build stronger relationships, both professionally and personally. With her vast global experience coaching top leaders, Gina lays out a step-by-step communicator. Don't just read it though; make sure to apply what Gina shares because once you do, you will flourish.

—Simon Alexander Ong
Life coach, business strategist,
bestselling author of Energize

Gina London's book is what we all need—an accessible, helpful, clear and effective book about how to use our own lives and life experiences to become more purposeful and conscious communicators. Gina weaves examples from her own vast professional experience through the book as she guides you to communicate with others in ways that will benefit you and them. This must-have book is filled with golden nuggets that will show you how to captivate and hold people's attention in your own unique way.

—Sinead Moriarty
Award-winning author of
eighteen novels published by Penguin Random House and
four children's books published by Gill

Amplify YOU

How to Connect More Powerfully in an AI World

Gina London

Foreword by Susan Scott, author of *Wall Street Journal* bestseller *Fierce Conversations*

WILEY

Published by John Wiley & Sons, Inc., Hoboken, New Jersey.

For general information on our other products and services or for technical support, please contact our Customer Care Department within the United States at (800) 762-2974, outside the United States at (317) 572-3993 or fax (317) 572-4002.

Wiley also publishes its books in a variety of electronic formats. Some content that appears in print may not be available in electronic formats. For more information about Wiley products, visit our web site at www.wiley.com.

Library of Congress Cataloging-in-Publication Data has been applied for:

ISBN: 9781394439058 (cloth)
ISBN: 9781394439065 (ePub)
ISBN: 9781394439072 (ePDF)

Cover Design: Wiley
Cover Image: coolvectormaker/stock.adobe.com
Author Photo: Courtesy of Shauna Kennedy

Printed and bound by CPI Group (UK) Ltd, Croydon, CR0 4YY

C9781394439058_100726

"An average human looks without seeing, listens without hearing, touches without feeling, eats without tasting, moves without physical awareness, inhales without awareness of odor or fragrance, and talks without thinking..."

—Leonardo da Vinci

"...This book can fix all that."

—Gina London

www.GinaLondon.com

To Fuchsia Fishbourne and Dave Pliler

for both initial and essential encouragement

Contents

Foreword

I admit that when some people start talking, I drift off. Not with Gina London. Never with Gina London. We met when she stepped off a float-plane on Orcas Island, off the coast of Washington state in the upper-left corner of the United States. Before we headed to my treehouse on top of a small mountain on the island, we had fish and chips at the marina with the sun on our faces. Pretty sure there were margaritas. I was struck by her presence, her poise, her character. My thought was, someone is here.

You may have felt that same thing when meeting someone for the first time. Perhaps, like me, you sat up a bit straighter, leaned in, paid fierce attention. Not even knowing exactly why you felt this way or what to expect, but having the feeling that something of import might be coming your way.

And then there are people, many, sad to say, who don't capture our attention. They may be perfectly wonderful, but the way they show up is tepid. Or fake.

Speaking is an art. It can be done poorly or well. It can be received poorly or well. It's the voice and the delivery. I'll come back to the voice, but what about the delivery? How do we get through to people who didn't necessarily turn up to hang on our every word? This book will show you how to deliver your message in a way that captures attention and enriches relationships, no matter the topic and no matter the setting, including a simple conversation. With Gina's permission, I want to bolt on a few thoughts of my own.

I've probably given at least 500 keynote talks, and I will share with you, immodestly I admit, the reasons that I am well received. Three reasons, really.

The first is humor. It's where I begin, and it's always sprinkled throughout my talks. Since my topic, the fact that our lives succeed or fail one conversation at a time, may not initially excite everyone in attendance, I often begin by disclosing that I don't want more conversations in my life. I want fewer conversations that actually accomplish something. So, when I'm seated next to a talker on an airplane, I excuse myself and leave a book with a fake cover on it, in plain view. The title: *Rebuilding Your Life After Federal Prison.* That usually does the trick. Heavenly silence for the rest of the flight.

The second reason has to do with emotion. The purpose of any speaking engagement—a meeting, a keynote, a podcast, an interview—must accomplish more than simply delivering data. The purpose of any talk is to evoke emotion, because without that, the message will not land. We are emotional creatures. Emotion provides the lit match something to ignite. I am passionate about my message and the difference it can make in people's lives, and so I have a great deal of emotion while I'm speaking, and it shows. I am not trying to please or impress. My aim is to connect, to touch people in some way.

Third, I am not talking to a vast room of people. I make eye contact with one person at a time throughout my talk and stay with each person until there is some acknowledgment that they have been seen, that they know I am talking to them. If it's a Zoom meeting, I imagine I'm talking to one person sitting across from me in my living room. After one talk, a woman came up to me and said that she had the sensation she had been seen, and she hadn't even known she'd felt invisible. That broke my heart.

Back to the voice. The actor Kathleen Turner worked on deepening her voice. If you haven't seen the movie *Body Heat*, you'll see what all the fuss is about. A deep, smoldering voice, so unlike the voices of most women. I'm not advocating for the smoldering part in most settings, but if you don't love what you hear when you listen to a recording of yourself, you can change it. Improve it.

Gina's voice is melodic. Her enunciation is perfect. Her attention, as we spoke that afternoon on Orcas Island, was unwavering, and if I remember right, we couldn't stop smiling at each other. We knew we were on to something good. During the following two days together, our conversations, on topics both professional and personal, bonded us for life.

E. M. Forster said, "The only books that influence us are those for which we are ready, and which have gone a little further down our particular path than we have yet got ourselves." Gina has gone way down the road and is reporting back. The stories from her career as a broadcaster and executive coach are riveting. Whether you are tasked with giving talks, making presentations to colleagues, meeting with your boss, or even conducting a family meeting to decide where to go on vacation, Gina is the best coach you could ever find.

There is so much to learn here. Gina points out that there is a difference between your whole self and your best self. Where is that best self of yours? Maybe you've hidden it under the proverbial bushel, or maybe you don't even recognize that there is a best self to access. As she says, you don't need to find your voice. You need to amplify it. I couldn't agree more.

—**Susan Scott**, author of *Fierce Conversations: Achieving Success at Work and in Life, One Conversation at a Time; Fierce Leadership: A Bold Alternative to the Worst "Best" Practices in Business Today*; and *Fierce Love: Creating a Love That Lasts, One Conversation at a Time*

Introduction

How Do You Bring Your Best Self to Work and Life?

With the meteoric rise of AI and other technology, your human skills are the core skills that will set you apart. But most of us take our communication for granted. We open our mouths, and words just come tumbling out. Sometimes we're focused; often, we're not. As leadership expert and bestselling author John Maxwell (whom I've met several times) writes, "*Everyone communicates. Few connect.*"

This book is based on my years as a network television reporter and two decades of experience coaching and training tens of thousands of people all over the world. It will help you become more confident and comfortable by teaching you *how* to take more control of how you communicate, in work and in life.

Many books tell you to bring your *whole* self to work and life. But there is a better way. I'm going to teach you how to bring your *best* self. Many books also focus on the *what* and the *why* of communication. For the "what," let's agree that communication is much more than its simple definition as "the transfer of information." For instance, your communications are rarely neutral; they are either building or dismantling your relationship with those you are communicating with. For the "why," I'm sure you're all familiar with Simon Sinek encouraging you to "Find your why." Of course, that's important. Why do I want to build and nurture relationships with other people? Why do I take time to truly listen, to connect, to show I care?

Why do I seek to understand before being understood? Because relationships are the foundation of influence. They build trust, unlock opportunities, and create the kind of connection that turns good intentions into great impact. So now that we understand the *what* and the *why*, I'm going to focus on the *how*.

It's not about bringing your whole self—it's about bringing your best self, on purpose.

When you choose to become a more purposeful and conscious communicator by using the tools and tips in this book, I guarantee you will build better relationships. You will evolve into a master at building relationships. You will become a better connector. You're not a robot; you're a human, and human skills are developable and learnable like anything else. Machine learning is encroaching on our very existence, so I'm convinced we need these skills more than ever before.

Imagine flipping a switch and filling a dark room with light. Before the room is brightened, you must decide to flip the switch, right? This book is about understanding the variety of choices we can make to better shine and share our individual light. Each of you has a light to share. You're likely currently communicating by *default*. I'll help you take more control to communicate by *design*. Over time, these approaches will become your new default.

Think of your possible communications progression this way:

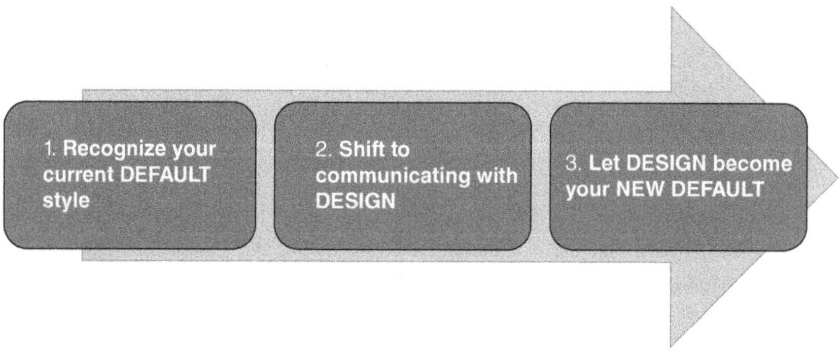

Becoming a communicator by design, or a purposeful and purpose-filled communicator, will improve all your relationships with colleagues, clients, neighbors, friends, and family.

When we communicate—whether it's a meeting, a conversation, or a presentation—so many things are happening at once. In this book, we'll break those elements down, one by one. We'll look at what they are, how they show up, and how you can use them more intentionally. Because once you understand *how* you're communicating, you gain the power to *choose* how you want to show up. And that's exactly what this book will help you explore.

I'm going to group these choices for you into three main categories. I like to chunk teaching tools as much as I can into sets of three because I think it's easier to remember and apply. It definitely works better that way for me. I'm the first to admit I'm not an academic. I'm a practitioner who likes to keep things simple. That said, I've had the privilege of validating my methods with some of the world's leading scholars. More importantly, I've developed these approaches by working across the globe with real people, just like you. So, here you go. I've distilled the way people experience communications into the three main sections of this book:

- **Say it!** (The way you talk to yourself and others.)
- **Look it!** (The messages you send through body language, grooming, and wardrobe.)
- **Be it!** (The practical behaviors and applications you can adapt to become a more positive and impactful communicator and connector.)

Imagine the three legs of a wooden stool. If only one leg is solid and the other two are split or wobbly, you will be out of balance and will eventually fall. We need all three to be sturdy and strong.

Within these three sections are a series of stories and lessons that will quickly and succinctly introduce you to the tools and techniques you can use to help you better connect—human to human. It doesn't matter who you are or where you are from, you can get great at this!

If I can do it, so can you.

I grew up in a small town in Indiana, and I've now visited more than fifty countries and lived in six of them. I was a little girl who spoke with a thick accent and had moments of extreme shyness. I've since interviewed presidents, a pope, a princess, and been recognized with an Emmy as a network correspondent and anchor. I've had the privilege of helping tens of thousands of people around the world become more confident and comfortable with how they tell their stories. I currently live in Ireland. And I'm a single mom.

Throughout my current work as a speaker, trainer, and executive coach, I have had the opportunity to support clients ranging from ordinary people seeking to be more successful to senior leaders of Fortune 100 companies who have already gained positions of power. You might think that business leaders must already be perfect connectors, but they're not.

One high-level leader I worked with was extremely successful in developing AI tools to drive marketing for his global beverage brand, but had never woven in a personal story when he presented before his team. Another was a seasoned finance expert and CFO of the European division of a multinational organization. He had mastered numbers, but not the stage. After two years of remote work during Covid, the thought of presenting in person to the entire sales division felt daunting. There was a South African plant manager for a pharmaceutical company who was one of the only female leaders of her kind in her region. She wanted more confidence in claiming her space during meetings and offering her opinions. One of my all-time favorite clients is the chief technology officer for a large global construction company. He initially reached out to me after a previous coach told him, "There's nothing more to teach you." He disagreed with that premise and said, "I want to continue polishing and improving even an extra one percent." As I'm writing this book, he remains a wonderful client. The most effective senior leaders are those who are humble and constantly refining themselves to ensure they're connecting the best way they can.

I'm also privileged to support thousands of middle managers in amplifying themselves. One of them was so filled with dread at the thought of being asked to stand and give an impromptu update on a project that he pretended to receive an emergency phone call from his wife and rushed out of the room rather than present before his colleagues. Another, in North Carolina, sheepishly admitted to me he had delivered a virtual presentation by monotonously reading his entire script while holding it under the camera on his laptop so he wouldn't forget what he wanted to say… or dare to trust himself to adlib. Then there was the young tech exec in Singapore who was asked to participate in a panel discussion for an industry conference. He was used to wearing jeans and a T-shirt and wanted recommendations for something to wear that still felt like him but also provided more of an air of authority. Since he had never sat on a panel before, he also didn't have a clue about what signals his body language could be sending.

I've also had the pleasure of coaching junior employees and even college students. One of the most gratifying interactive webinars I was hired for was Oracle's "Bring Your Family to Work Day" in Southeast Asia. I took the stage twice at The Edge Summit for thousands of students from Lagos, Nigeria, and I've been the emcee for Cork University's business school's annual conference in Ireland more times than I can remember. Oh, and I've had the extreme honor of working with the International Children's Peace Prize committee, participants, and winners for four years.

No matter what age, industry, country, or level of seniority and experience, there is a consistent thread or desire among each of these people. They all want to take more control—to more positively impact, connect, persuade, and influence their colleagues, their employees, their boards, and even themselves.

The key to success lies in understanding the *choices* you can make to connect more purposely. The first step toward building better and stronger connections comes when you heighten your own awareness of how you currently communicate. Most people would say they're decent communicators, but when they dig deeper, they admit they could take more control.

I provide my clients a pre-assessment form before we first work together to get a baseline of their opinions about themselves and their leadership communications impact. Most people initially give themselves pretty high marks. After our work together, I provide them with a similar post-assessment form. I find that those same people often grade themselves *lower* the second time around. It's not because they've gotten worse, but because their awareness has increased—both about themselves and the opportunities before them—to take greater control of how they strategize, structure, and deliver their communications, allowing them to become even more impactful.

It's like flipping on a light in a dark room—everything changes with a single choice. And you've already made one by picking up this book.

Thank you for making the choice to take more control of how you connect with other humans.

When you choose to become a more purposeful, conscious, and focused communicator by using the tools and strategies that I will share with you, I guarantee you will become a more confident and comfortable communicator. You will become a better human connector. You will be able to fill a dark room with light and do so more comfortably. Better connections with those you work and interact with will amplify the energy between you. And these connections will create an invaluable bond of trust between you that will benefit you both. The way to achieve this is to first understand the steps that happen when people experience communication. These steps inform the structure of this book, chapter by chapter.

As I've said, I've traveled from Indiana to India, Atlanta to Athens, London to Lagos, and Switzerland to Saudi Arabia—working in more than fifty countries and thousands of cities. Along the way, I've partnered with college students, junior employees, middle managers, and CEOs of global companies. No matter where they're from or what title they hold, they share one thing: a desire to make a positive impact.

I have put a lot of my experience into every page, and you'll get a lot out of it if you simply invest a little time and effort.

Making This Book Work for You

The experience of reading this book is meant to be interactive. You will see QR codes sprinkled throughout. Scan these codes, and they will bring you to me via video tutorials, where you'll experience the power of connection with me to understand the communication choices you can make. Using these QR codes will help you maximize this book's potential… and your potential.

Purposeful communication is not just about making a one-off presentation or speech better, though it will do that too. It's a lifestyle choice; a leadership-style choice; a human-to-human choice. Let me say this again:

Purposeful communication is a choice.

ChatGPT and other AI tools are fantastic for tasks, but until the robots take over, *only we humans have the power to take more control of how we connect person to person.* Again, this applies not only to work but also to every facet of our daily lives.

"We don't have a professional life and a personal life. We just have a life."

—Alan Weiss

I heartily agree with this quote. I've read several books by Alan Weiss. Years ago, when I was living in Tuscany, I learned he and his wife were vacationing in Florence. He agreed to meet with me. We had coffee in the lobby of the Four Seasons hotel, where they were staying. Much later, when I moved to Dublin, I interviewed him for the weekly business and leadership column for the newspaper I still write for here in my adopted home of Ireland. (It's called *The Sunday Independent*, and it's the widest read in the country.) I've learned plenty from Alan, and as a lifelong learner, I know I can learn something from everyone I meet.

One day, I hope to meet each of you. I hope you learn something from this book, and I also hope you'll reach out to me to let me know how you've improved. Remember, you're already communicating every day. I hope you get excited about heightening your awareness of how you communicate, so you can better connect.

Think of this book as a set of golf clubs, tools in your toolkit, or spices in your pantry. Once you understand the difference between a two-iron and a nine-iron, a wrench and pliers, or tarragon and thyme, you'll feel more confident and comfortable choosing the right communication and connection tools at the right time to achieve better results.

As one of my favorite coaching clients said to me after we had completed our work together. "You didn't change me; you amplified me." That's exactly the point. You already have a voice. Together, we can *amplify* it with purpose. Here's to better connections in your work and life!

Every kindness,

Gina

The Top Ten Questions

What Leaders Ask When They're Ready to Grow

Before we dive into the stories and strategies ahead, I want to share ten of the most thoughtful—and frequently asked—questions I've received from clients over the years. These questions go straight to the heart of the technique I'll teach you, called *The Amplify Approach*: how we show up, how we connect, and how we grow into the most confident, compassionate version of ourselves, at work and beyond.

After each question, you'll find honest, practical answers designed to challenge assumptions, spark reflection, and set the tone for what's ahead. Whether you're a seasoned executive, an emerging leader, or somewhere in between, these Q&As will help you start thinking—and communicating—with greater clarity, purpose, and presence.

1. **Client:** *I agree with your approach and techniques, but it's too hard for me to be consistent. Where should I start?*
   Gina: Most worthwhile things are not easy, but consistency starts small. Begin by journaling and focusing on one actionable area, like

making a habit of not interrupting others and actively listening with engaged facial expressions. Celebrate your progress, no matter how small. This is a lifetime endeavor. Life is full of setbacks, so take it one moment at a time.

2. **Client:** *Don't you think all this seems like we're trying way too hard to please everyone else?*
   Gina: I prefer to see it as compassionate, thoughtful, and intentional. Choosing to create a positive communication experience for you and others. It's about respect and kindness, not buzzwords. It takes strength of character to prioritize others' perspectives while remaining authentic. Isn't building meaningful relationships worth the effort?

3. **Client:** *What about my ego? I don't want to come across as weak, and I also don't want to be perceived as too forceful or self-important.*
   Gina: That's such an important question—and one I hear often. Many people assume that speaking with authority means sounding domineering or "in charge" in a way that pushes others aside. But true authority doesn't come from volume or ego—it comes from clarity, calm, and care.

   It's natural to be thinking, "*Am I doing okay? Do I seem confident? Is this landing?*" That's human. But here's the paradox: the more we focus on making others feel seen, heard, and respected, the more confident and compelling we actually become.

   Authority and compassion are not opposites. In fact, the strongest communicators lead with both. You don't need to be loud to be powerful. You need to be intentional, present, and kind. That's what people remember—and respond to.

4. **Client:** *Some leaders don't lead in the way you coach yet still succeed. What about them?*
   Gina: I agree that "command-and-control" leadership can yield short-term results, but the cracks show during crises. Leaders who rely on fear or compliance often find themselves alone when the stakes are highest. Collaborative, empathetic leadership builds loyalty, resilience, and trust for the long haul.

5. **Client:** *I just want to be me. Why should I work so hard to become something I'm not?*
   Gina: That's wonderful—you should be authentically you. But remember, growth is a natural part of life. The Amplify Approach is about bringing out the best version of yourself in different situations. Self-acceptance and self-development aren't opposites; they complement each other beautifully.

6. **Client:** *Isn't focusing on things like body language and wardrobe superficial?*
   Gina: Not at all. These are tools to communicate respect, intention, and confidence before you even speak. When you pay attention to these elements, you're not being shallow—you're demonstrating that you value your audience's time and attention. First impressions matter, and how you present yourself sets the tone for deeper connections.

7. **Client:** *I'm shy and introverted. Won't these techniques feel unnatural for me?*
   Gina: Many of my clients are introverted and find these tools incredibly empowering. The Amplify Approach isn't about changing your personality; it's about aligning your words, voice, and body language with your authentic self. Start with small steps that feel manageable, like practicing in front of a mirror or recording yourself to build confidence.

8. **Client:** *Isn't this advice more relevant to extroverts who naturally thrive in communication?*
   Gina: This is similar to question number seven, so let me be clear: extroverts and introverts alike benefit from these strategies. Introverts often have a quieter strength that can shine through when amplified with intention. Extroverts can often benefit from consciously creating more structure and guardrails around their free-spirited style of communication. It's not about being loud; it's about being impactful, no matter your style. This book is about *amplifying your strengths.*

9. **Client:** *What if I try these techniques and people still don't respond well to me?*
   Gina: Remember, communication is a two-way street. You can't control every reaction, but you can control how you present yourself.

If something doesn't land, reflect, adapt, and try again. The Amplify Approach isn't about perfection—it's about progress and building deeper, more meaningful relationships over time. That said, become proficient with any of these techniques and strategies, and it will amplify you. Guaranteed. I've seen it work over and over.

10. **Client:** *Won't people see through these techniques and view them as manipulative?*
    Gina: The Amplify Approach isn't about manipulation; it's about being intentional and respectful in how you connect with others. If your intent is genuine and you sincerely strive for a mutually beneficial outcome, people will feel it. These techniques are simply tools to help you express yourself in a way that better resonates with those around you.

PART 1 Say It!

1 The Comparison Trap

How to Take More Control of What You Say to Others and Yourself

"The happiness of your life depends upon the quality of your thoughts."

—Marcus Aurelius

Someone Always Has a Bigger Boat…

A BAGPIPER WAS GOING TO PLAY.

I was sitting in the green room at the Disney Institute in Florida as the show's organizer reviewed the program rundown with me. It was only my first year as an anchor at CNN, and it was a huge honor to have been invited to serve as Master of Ceremonies for an event they were calling "A Day of Peace."

Two thousand people gathered at the institute's large conference center to listen to two of the world's top thinkers on the topic: Nobel Peace Prize winners Oscar Arias and Archbishop Desmond Tutu. As Costa Rica's president, Oscar Arias had won the award for organizing a regional peace plan for strife-torn Central America. Desmond Tutu won for his efforts to end apartheid in South Africa.

As I listened to the woman talk me through the activities for the day, I may have appeared calm on the outside, but inside, I was a bag of nerves.

The year was 2000—I was still quite young and not a seasoned, experienced television presenter. As MC for the event, it was my duty to welcome everyone in attendance and then facilitate an hour-long fireside chat that just happened to be with a couple of the greatest minds on the planet. All that, *and* then the show's organizer told me there would be a professional bagpiper to lead us during the opening processional. The four of us were to walk down the main aisle through the audience, and then, while the bagpiper stood to one side below the platform and continued to play, the three of us would ascend the stairs onto the stage and start the event.

I don't know why the image of some man wearing that formal Scottish Highlands uniform with the dark plaid kilt and big black feather bonnet, slowly marching while the bagpipes wailed their mournful cry, sent me over the edge, but it did. I was smiling and nodding my head at her while secretly clenching and unclenching my hands under the table. I was overwhelmed. *How am I going to rise to this occasion?*

I was still trying to collect my thoughts after the organizer walked away when I noticed someone new heading over to me. It was Costa Rica's president, Oscar Arias. While I was engaged with the event director, he and his handlers were standing in one corner of the room talking, and the archbishop and his team were holding court on the opposite side of the room. Each group had arrived about twenty minutes earlier. President Arias and his gang were rather subdued and quiet when they entered and introduced themselves. In contrast, as soon as the broadly smiling archbishop came through the door of the green room, he exuberantly, even playfully, greeted me and every person in the room, shaking every hand. It was my first time meeting him, and he absolutely radiated charm and magnetic energy.

His energy clearly impacted the other Nobel Prize winner in the room because, when Oscar Arias approached me, he spoke softly under his breath, "Help me. What can I do compared to the big-big-big style of that man?"

I remember being instantly shaken out of my own thoughts of uncertainty to focus instead on the man standing before me. He was the former leader of a nation and a recipient of the top peace prize in the world, yet he also was struggling with self-doubt. He was comparing himself unfavorably in the light of someone else.

I encouraged him to lean into the power of his personal style as a reserved, thoughtful man. "Be proud of your own unique story and share that," I said.

You can do the same.

… Just Sail Yours

When it comes to communication—and life in general—one of the quickest ways to sink your confidence is to compare yourself to others. My favorite illustration of this is a metaphor of a boat that I learned from reading a book by Alan Weiss.

Weiss once wrote, "There is always a bigger boat" (TIAABB). He meant the same thing we've all felt when we look at someone else's résumé, social media feed, or speaking style and think: They have a yacht or a cruise ship compared to my little rowboat. *I'll never measure up.*

Weiss tells the story of being invited aboard a client's impressive sixty-five-foot yacht. As he admired it, he noticed an even bigger, more luxurious vessel docked nearby. Suddenly, the yacht he was standing on looked small.

That moment captures what happens when we compare ourselves. No matter how capable we are, there will always be someone with more experience, more followers, or a flashier presentation style. And if we let ourselves focus on that, we miss the value of our own strengths.

I've seen this play out in my own life. Like most siblings, I've long compared myself to my brother Brad. As chance would have it, he literally works with boats. For his yacht restoration business, he has refitted everything from J. K. Rowling's yacht to President Kennedy's *Honey Fitz*. It's hard to imagine anyone more at the top of his game than my brother. But instead of doubting myself in comparison—or wishing I could afford one of the yachts he works on—I remind myself that if I could only afford to buy a canoe, it still floats and is seaworthy in its own way.

And so it is with communication. Maybe you're not the flashiest speaker on the stage. Maybe your voice shakes a little when you start. That doesn't mean you don't belong in the water. What matters is whether your message carries people from one point to another.

The message is simple: there's always a bigger boat. But that fact doesn't diminish yours—it only proves that comparison is a losing game. Your job as a communicator isn't to have the biggest boat. It's to know your boat, steer it well, and trust that it can make the journey.

Your Story Has the Power to Impact Someone

When you start a personal development journey, it has to be because you want to improve your confidence and comfort to connect better with others by bringing forward the best version of you. Not because you are competing with or comparing yourself to someone else.

In 2019, I was again in Orlando. This time, I wasn't going to be on stage facilitating a conversation between two global leaders. Instead, I was attending a leadership conference as an eager participant. I was sitting in a darkened ballroom in the World Center Marriott, listening to bestselling leadership author John Maxwell deliver the keynote address. Two people seated next to me, who appeared to be in their mid-thirties, were whispering to each other about how hearing him speak made them feel more intimidated than empowered. I found that disappointing. Here were two young people feeling inadequate next to a seasoned expert with more than fifty years of experience.

Comparisons like this are unfair—and unhelpful. If you're still honing your skills, don't measure yourself against someone at the peak of their career. Growth takes time, and every expert was once a beginner.

Later in the same year, I was in Stockholm leading a storytelling workshop with the senior leadership team from the Absolut company. As I was encouraging each leader to take five minutes to jot down a personal story they would like to weave into an upcoming business presentation, I was surprised when one participant looked up at me. She confided, "I never tell personal stories because I've never done anything interesting." How sad she thought that way. Of course she had interesting stories to tell. I believe we need to see ourselves with more awareness, yes, but not with more self-limiting beliefs or self-criticism.

One of my earliest coaching clients, who is now a fantastic private executive coach, was working as sales director for CompTIA (the global

IT certification company) when I met him. When I first urged him to start blogging and sharing stories about his experience managing global teams, he hesitated. "I don't know. I really don't think of myself as an expert." Just as with the Absolut executive, he needed to change his mindset and stop comparing himself to others who were already describing themselves as "experts."

In my experience, most so-called experts become known as experts because, over many years, they have learned to step forward and share their stories.

You Are the Expert of Your Life

You don't need to be a best-selling author like John Maxwell. You don't need to be a movie star, an astronaut, or have successfully scaled Mount Everest on a pogo stick to have a story to tell. You definitely don't need to win a Nobel Prize.

You are the expert in your life. And I know your life is full of stories. Right now. Many times, in fact, it's the more ordinary stories, like when you tried to ride a bike for the first time or when you watched your child take their first steps, that will more meaningfully connect with other people. In my experience, people more readily relate to our everyday stories than the rarer tales of the extraordinary.

Of course, that doesn't mean you can't take inspiration from those great-storied celebrities or athletes out there who have exceptional talent or exude extraordinary presence.

I just want to remind you that when any powerful speaker or influential leader comes to mind, use your assessment of those people to *propel* your practice, not to *deter* you from it. While comparisons are part of the human condition, they don't have to be negative. In fact, they can be a source of inspiration, a spark that propels you to find your own way and write your own story. The challenge is resisting the urge to let those comparisons diminish your sense of self-worth.

You Already Have a Voice

In 2018, I was asked to facilitate a brainstorming conference of the top global contributors to UNICEF. The children's humanitarian organization had convened a diverse range of individual donors under one roof in

Florence, Italy, to explore how they might combine their financial forces to tackle a single, large project together.

Besides fostering the conversations among and between the participants, I also introduced each of the compelling young speakers. The organizers had invited these incredible young people to share their personal stories of how UNICEF had impacted their lives. One young man stood out to me. He talked about how he had been conscripted into a guerilla militant group in Sierra Leone when he was just a boy. Fortunately, he escaped and managed to make his way to a UNICEF refugee camp. Sponsors there helped him complete his schooling and enroll in a university.

"UNICEF gave you a voice," one donor remarked after the young man had concluded his presentation.

"No," he kindly, yet firmly, corrected them. And then he responded with this:

"I was born with a voice. You helped me amplify it."

I thought his words were powerful and they stuck with me. The difference between what the donor said and how the young man responded. Perhaps it's a subtle distinction. But whoever you are, I want you to know I appreciate you and the voice you already have. The comment from the young man at the UNICEF event is similar to the compliment I already mentioned in the Introduction—the one I received from that coaching client as we wrapped up our engagement, who told me: "You didn't change me; you *amplified* me." This is it. I want to recognize and celebrate with you—the life you've led up to now. The people you've met. The conversations you've had. The speeches you've given. Your successes. Your disappointments. You.

All your experiences so far have led you to this moment, and to this book. Let's explore how to *amplify* you together.

The Starfish Parable

There's a parable that beautifully illustrates the importance of focusing on our individual impact rather than being overwhelmed by the vastness of the world around us. Maybe you've heard it already, but even if you have, I think it bears repeating.

> *One early morning, a child arrived at the beach to discover it had become littered with thousands of starfish which had washed ashore. Without a word, the child began to carefully pick them up, one by one, tossing each back into the sea.*
>
> *A man walking by watched for a while before calling out, "Why bother? You can't possibly make a difference to all of those starfish."*
>
> *The child briefly looked at the man and considered his words. Then the child bent down again, picked up another starfish, and threw it back into the water. Then, with a simple smile, the child said, "But I made a difference to that one, didn't I?"*

I first heard this story when I was a child myself, growing up in Indiana, and before I had ever stepped on a sandy ocean beach. Now that I live in Ireland, our home is only about a five-minute walk from Dublin Bay. At low tide, it's a joy when I can convince my teenage daughter Lulu to join me in taking our mini schnauzer Pepper for a walk on the beach. We've never seen a starfish there, but we do see plenty of discarded razor clamshells and I never get tired of the experience of walking on the sand.

Of course, regardless of whether you have ever strolled on a beach, I hope the parable resonates as deeply with you as it does with me. I know how easy it is to feel overwhelmed by the sheer scale of challenges we may face, both personally and professionally. We look around and see others who seem to be achieving so much, while we may feel like we're just tossing a few starfish back into the sea, hoping it makes a difference. But our efforts matter, even if we only reach one person. We don't need to change the entire world in a single moment; we just need to make a difference for *one*. That one can be you.

The Negative Comparison Trap

It's completely normal to compare yourself to others, but it's worth knowing that this habit can take a real toll on your mental health and productivity. Research in psychology, including the well-known social comparison theory by Leon Festinger, shows that constantly measuring yourself against others can trigger feelings of anxiety and self-doubt. And often, you may not even notice how much it's affecting you.

Here's the important thing to remember: it's not the comparison itself that causes harm—it's how you *choose* to interpret it. When you see someone else's success, you have a choice. You can let it make you feel like you're falling short, or you can choose to see it as a sign that big things are possible—and use it as inspiration for your own growth.

This is why mindset is so crucial. If we approach comparisons with a growth mindset—the belief we can improve and evolve—then seeing someone else succeed can become a powerful motivator. On the flip side, if we approach them with a fixed mindset, where we believe our abilities are set in stone, then other people's success or their dynamic presenting becomes a threat and a reminder of our perceived limitations.

Let's resolve not to judge our lives by looking at others—TIAABB! Instead, together, I want to explore and uplift your life as it is right now. When we start to unpack the components of how we currently communicate and connect with others, we must start with ourselves.

Your Story Matters

Whether you're leading a team, managing a project, or simply trying to make sense of your own path, your experiences, your voice, and your perspective matter.

I've had the privilege of working with countless leaders over the years, and what I've learned is that it's not about being the most charismatic or the most accomplished on paper. It's about being authentic, about showing up with the courage to share who you are, not who you think others want you to be.

Think about the last time someone told you a story that moved you. Was it because they were the most polished speaker? Or was it because their message resonated with something deep inside you? More often than not, it's the latter. We connect with vulnerability, with honesty, and with the shared human experience of triumphs and struggles.

Your story doesn't need to be grand or world-changing to matter. It just needs to be *yours*. And if it impacts even one person, if it helps someone else feel seen or understood, then it's worth telling.

I want you to take a moment and imagine who you are right now. Think about your experiences. Your impact. Your communications. Your connections. Your voice. Close your eyes for one minute and just reflect.

Now open your eyes, and without comparing yourself to anyone else, pick a number on the number line below.

With the number 10 representing consistent accuracy and perfection, and number 1 standing for the least confident and comfortable you feel, pick the number you think best matches your current level of confidence and comfort around your abilities. How purposefully and carefully you are taking control of how you communicate and connect. How you exude and *amplify* the best version of you. This number is your starting point.

Be honest. For instance, I've been working in this leadership communications field for nearly two decades now—more if you count my previous journalism career—and I am certainly not a perfect 10. But I am making steps toward improving myself, and you can too. I try daily to remember not to compare myself negatively with others. It's hard, what with all the seemingly perfect people out there sharing their perfect homes, vacations, families, and bodies on social media. Right? I believe it takes a daily decision to reset our intentions—whether that's first thing in the morning or just before we go to sleep at night.

I'm sure we will all continue to have moments of feeling like the smaller boat in the marina. But what if, instead of wishing for a bigger vessel, we learned to appreciate the strength and beauty of our own? What if, instead of comparing ourselves to others, we focus on how our unique gifts can make a difference?

The next time you find yourself comparing, pause for a moment. Remember the child and the starfish. Remember Oscar Arias and Desmond Tutu. After our conversation that day in the green room, I remember he took the stage with a quiet, steady confidence. Instead of trying to match the archbishop's vibrant energy, Oscar shared a story from his childhood—a simple, powerful memory that sparked his lifelong commitment to improving Costa Rica. His calm yet resolute presence spoke volumes, capturing the audience's attention in a way that was uniquely him.

Afterward, when I told him how moving his message was, he smiled, and with a newfound ease, said, "I felt more comfortable in my own skin." That moment can become a reminder to us all: The greatest strength we can bring to any stage, any challenge, is an unwavering sense of self. The only story you need to tell is your own, and that's more than enough to make a difference.

Make a positive commitment to be the best you can be. That commitment is to you, from you.

The trouble is, you didn't put every thought about yourself into your head. A lot of what has become our own self-talk was first put there by someone else. Are you ready to examine that? Then let's begin.

You Are Who You Think You Are

Before you turn the page to Chapter 2, if you have ever struggled with the comparison trap, please scan the QR code for another reminder of why you and your unique story truly matter.

2 Self-Talk

Inner Critic or Inner Coach?

The First Person You Talk to Every Morning and the Last Person You Talk to Every Night Is... You

The First Person You Talk To

I WAS AFRAID TO KNOCK ON THE DOOR.

When I was eight years old, I stood outside the front door of Mr. Halderman's house. A little red wagon was next to me, filled with boxes of Girl Scout cookies. This is still a familiar ritual for many young American girls going door to door selling cookies like Trefoils, Peanut Butter Sandwiches, and Thin Mints to raise money for scouting activities.

My mom was waiting at the bottom of the driveway for me to get on with it. But my hand was frozen at my side. Delivering a sales pitch is challenging for most people, but especially when you're a child about to try to sell to the scariest grown-up on the block. I don't remember exactly why Mr. Halderman intimidated me so much—other than he was big, scary, and hairy. No, seriously, he just came across as kind of rough and unfriendly. But since Mom and I were making our way methodically to every home in our neighborhood, it wasn't an option to skip his house. So there I was, staring up at his door.

I finally mustered the nerve and tapped quietly. I hoped he either wasn't home or wouldn't hear me, and I could turn around and leave. But the door swung open, and I found myself looking up at his scowling face. At least that's what I imagined. What I do remember is this. Because of my nerves, I rushed through my sales pitch at lightning speed: "Would-ja-like-ta-buy-some-Girl-Scout-cookies?"

What he said next is seared into my memory. I can still hear his voice and feel how it dissolved my self-esteem the way a Girl Scout cookie would dissolve in hot, bitter coffee.

"What did you say? I couldn't understand a word you said," Mr. Halderman proclaimed. "You mumbled. In fact, I'm going to call you Mumbles from now on."

And he did.

For the following ten years that I lived in the Wolf's Wooded Acres neighborhood of Farmland, Indiana, until I graduated from high school, any time Mr. Halderman saw me, he called out, "Hey, Mumbles!"

It was mortifying and humiliating. I remember walking to school the long way around our neighborhood to avoid his house. What's worse, I don't think he even bought any cookies.

Developing "Executive Presence"

In 2010, I was in Waldorf, Germany, inside the impressive glass and steel headquarters of SAP, the global software company. I was meeting with my first corporate clients: three senior executives who were outlining their goals for our upcoming six-day coaching engagement.

"We want media, presentation, and executive presence training," one said.

As they shared the first item on their list, media training, I thought confidently, *No problem, I got this.*

I had finished my career in TV news broadcasting with more than a decade of experience under my belt. I had conducted thousands of interviews with politicians, celebrities, athletes, and newsworthy regular people. I was certain I could train these three guys how to field questions from the press effectively. I also felt quite comfortable teaching them how to create and deliver more impactful presentations, which was the second item on their list of goals. Throughout my tenure as a journalist, which began in newspapers, I had written countless articles and scripts. I was sure I could help them construct content that was memorable and rehearse delivery techniques designed to better captivate an audience.

But when they mentioned the third item on their list: "to improve their executive presence," I faltered. The self-conscious cookie-selling Mumbles girl inside me began feeling nervous again. Looking back, I know it was that emotional shudder of self-doubt known as imposter syndrome. I thought, *I hope they don't find me out*, as I smiled outwardly and nodded as a show of reassurance. After that, the initial priorities and goal-setting meeting was over, and the three execs departed. The first thing I did was hop on the internet and google the words "executive presence." It was the first time I had ever heard the term.

You see, throughout my tenure in the journalism industry—first in newspapers, then over to TV news—any notion of people management skills, human-centric culture, or creating some sort of an intentional atmosphere of professionalism was nowhere to be found. If you've watched programs depicting busy newsrooms around the 1990s and early 2000s, I'm here to tell you they're largely spot on. Back in those days, producers, directors, assignment editors, and other managers pretty much just yelled and bossed people around. I've heard from my former colleagues and friends who are still in the business that, except for sexual harassment now largely being a no-no, the environment is still pretty much the same.

Competency vs. Warmth

Executive presence is thankfully not simply about bossing people around. It's not something that's reserved only for so-called executives, either. I hope you already understand that this book is for everyone.

Exuding executive presence is about learning how to harness the power of you.

It's not command and control. It's developing the kind of leadership style that gets things done while simultaneously leaving a lasting, positive impact. It's learning how to give off a poised, I'll-be-your-gracious-host kind of feeling you might imagine receiving from the person who greets you at the door of a well-organized dinner party.

Once you discover and adapt the tools to become someone who effectively and consistently demonstrates executive presence, you are the person who strikes that rare balance between the two factors researchers say are the foundational characteristics required to build trust: *competency* and *warmth*.[1] You can sense this balance when they enter a room, run a meeting, or influence a team.

Like my first clients who sought to layer on this balance, please join me in understanding and accepting that executive presence is not a magical trait that some lucky people are simply born with. It's a combination of training and strategic choices that are activated by implementing what I describe as my ADD principle.

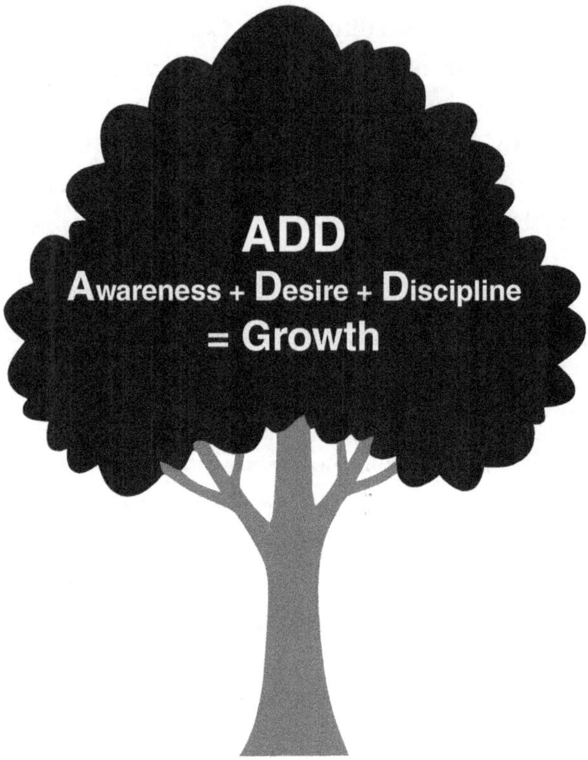

A. First, you must raise your **awareness** about who you are and how others perceive you. Who do I think I am? How do I actually behave? What vibes do I give off? What do I say when I'm under pressure? This book will help you sort through these questions and many more. Not to make you feel overwhelmed, but to allow you to unpack and repack with more purpose and control.

D. Next, armed with that awareness, you must stoke a real **desire** for personal and professional development. I want to stress that this holistic approach to developing your human connections is *not* the old, worn-out, fake-it-till-you-make-it idea. Real, genuine desire begins when you realize something powerful: You have more control than you might think.

You can choose how you show up—how you behave, how you communicate—in any situation.

And when you start to imagine the positive impact those choices can have on the people around you, that's when the excitement kicks in. There's nothing fake about real intentions. If you truly see the opportunity you have before you in your life to uplift others and forge deeper connections, that's not fake. That's real. I'm not talking about manipulating others for nefarious intentions, of course. As Stuart Diamond writes in his book *Getting More*,[2] when you're focused on obtaining mutually beneficial outcomes between yourself and the other person or people with whom you're dealing, that's a positive, not a negative approach.

D. Adapting these skills and characteristics will take some work. Awareness and desire are not enough. Like any effort, you will get more out of it depending on what you put into it. If you're truly excited about becoming the best version of yourself—and making a more positive impact on others and your own life—it doesn't just happen with the wave of a wand. There's no instant fix. It takes intention, effort, and consistency.

Imagine you want to learn to play a new musical instrument. You'll perform more quickly and effectively if you **discipline** yourself to practice every day. Change is not an intellectual exercise—we must *do* something differently. It's not merely thinking differently; it's putting new characteristics and strategies into action.

Who Do You Think You Are?

My first three clients from SAP, like thousands of people after them, began applying my ADD principle by looking inward. The first step is self-awareness. Let's explore this together. I want you to discover more about you. How aware are you about you? Write down seven words or phrases that come to mind to describe yourself. Don't overthink it; just write whatever pops into your head.

How Would I Describe Myself?

1. ____________________
2. ____________________
3. ____________________
4. ____________________
5. ____________________
6. ____________________
7. ____________________

Now, let's examine the words. What words do you know for certain were first put in there by you? And what words were put there by the Haldermans in your life?

Whether it's well-intended or mean-spirited, early words said by a neighbor, a coach, a teacher, a sibling, a peer, or a parent can have real, lasting power. Some comments may encourage us or remind us of characteristics we want to embrace, celebrate, and nurture.

> "You're very *curious*."
> "You're *hard-working*."
> "You're *resourceful*."
> "You're *independent*."
> "You've got a *great singing voice*."

But other observations, which may have been initially uttered in a careless, off-hand manner by the deliverer, may still be swirling around in your thoughts years and years later. Even if the observation was based only on a brief snapshot of you a long time ago, somehow, the words have taken root, and you now accept them as truth.

> "You're *too shy*."
> "You're *high-strung*."
> "You're *careless*."
> "You *can't sing*."

Sound familiar? Now, go back and examine the list of words you used to describe yourself. Are they words that serve you, or have you become a servant to them?

Understanding Negative Self-Talk: Where Does It Come From?

As with the seemingly offhand comment from my grouchy neighbor, the roots of your negative self-talk may trace back further than you realize.

Perhaps you were a young student diligently working through a math problem, struggling to find the right answer. Your teacher, perhaps overworked or simply unaware, sighed and said to you, "Math is just not your thing, is it?" To you as a child, just like me as that eight-year-old cookie sales rep, that statement wasn't just an off-hand comment. It could easily become an internalized belief that grows with time.

Or maybe you were that would-be athlete, only to be constantly reminded by your coach, "You're too timid; you'll never make the team." Every missed pass or hesitation on the field reinforces this statement. What starts as an external comment becomes an internal dialogue—"I'm not good enough." "I'm timid." And so, the words take root.

Whether it's a neighbor, a teacher, a parent, or a coach, these seemingly harmless remarks can plant the seeds of doubt. They embed themselves in our psyche, shape how we see ourselves, and ultimately become the lens through which we view the world. The challenge?

Many of us don't even recognize that many of our negative beliefs are not our own.

They're borrowed opinions, yet they govern our choices and, most important of all, *limit our potential.*

I mentioned briefly in the last chapter a wonderful coaching client of mine based in South Africa. She was the first female manufacturing plant manager in the region for a large pharmaceutical organization. Pretty much everyone would consider her a success. But she came to me because, despite her accomplishments, she still struggled to speak up in meetings.

"It's not that the other male managers are doing anything to make me feel insecure," she explained during one of our coaching sessions. "I think I keep hearing my father's voice comparing me to my two older brothers, who were much more outgoing and athletic than I was."

Another coaching client is the CEO of a large multinational paper products company. He has never enjoyed presenting before his employees, even though he knows they look forward to hearing from him.

"My mom made me perform on stage in a talent show when I was seven," he recalled. "I forgot my lines and my dance steps. I was so embarrassed. I have never enjoyed speaking in front of any group since."

My lovely friend Kate is one of the smartest women I know. She's well-spoken, a world traveler, and an avid reader. Yet, over lunch recently, she shared that she always wished she could sing, but because a teacher told her in grade school that she didn't have a "good voice," she didn't even try. What a shame.

I'm no psychologist, but I hear this theme all the time. Somebody's self-talk about their abilities or characteristics or style or worth is often connected to an early experience or someone else's assessment of them during their childhood. Wherever, whenever, and whomever those experiences and descriptions came from that are not serving you, it's time to identify them for what they are and root them out.

The Self-Fulfilling Prophecy of Negative Self-Talk

When we accept these negative scripts, we reinforce them over and over, creating what's known as a self-fulfilling prophecy. If you believe you're not good at public speaking, chances are you'll avoid opportunities to speak in front of others. And because you avoid it, you never practice, so when you do speak, you're unprepared, anxious, and confirm that you're not good at it.

The science behind this is grounded in cognitive psychology, the science of how we think. Simply put, our thoughts create emotions which drive our actions. If we believe that we're inadequate, we behave in ways that ensure we don't rise above that perceived inadequacy. It's like having blinders on that keep us from seeing the full picture. We don't take risks, we don't stretch ourselves, and we become trapped in a cycle of negative reinforcement.

But what if we could stop this vicious cycle? What if, instead of allowing these old scripts to dictate our choices, we started taking *control* of our own narrative?

Crafting Oars for Your Boat

It's important here to acknowledge how most of us live our lives. Most of us are like a rowboat out at sea, without an oar or paddle. When it comes to taking control of our careers, our relationships, or our lives, we're often adrift. Floating along. Pushed in whatever direction the wind is blowing. We don't prepare properly. We don't stop to think. We are really just reacting, not consciously planning.

But while we're floating along, we are still sending signals to others. We are communicating. Always.

Let's say that again:

We are never not communicating. Our communication teaches people how they should think about how we think we are.

Best-selling author Susan Scott writes about this in her book, *Fierce Love*. She's also written *Fierce Conversations* and *Fierce Leadership*, and I encourage you to check them out. I had the privilege of spending a couple of glorious days visiting with her at her treehouse retreat on Orcas Island in Washington State. I slept in the guest cabin nestled nearby on the ground, but I climbed up to her honest-to-goodness, life-sized, story-book-style treehouse to share meals and stories with Susan and her two dear little dogs. It was 2021, and it was an unforgettable experience.

But the first time I remember being taught the principle that we are responsible for teaching people how to treat us was in 2014. I was on a speaking circuit around Nigeria with the incomparable Richie Dayo Johnson.

RDJ, as his friends called him, was a tower of leadership power. Not only because of his tall, imposing stature, but also due to the exemplary executive presence demonstrated whenever he opened his mouth. Born in Nigeria and educated in London, he spoke with a booming lilt that was almost theatrical.

"Jolly good to meet you," he said when we were first introduced. I wondered if he was serious. I assure you, he was.

He sprinkled his conversations and presentations with maxims and adages that were catchy and meant to teach a lesson and impart a greater meaning. But it was more than performance. RDJ consistently walked his talk. Over the years, I grew to love and respect him for it.

In July 2020, when the world was in lockdown, we took part in a virtual conference that connected speakers and participants from all parts of the world to talk about the importance of speaking with intention.

It had been a while since we last saw each other and with Covid, who knew when we would see each other again? I texted him the following morning, "It was an honor to be in the same virtual room with you again, my brother."

He texted me back in his characteristic style, "I'm deeply touched by this. Let's continue to encourage each other by sharing more opportunities for growth and development. Welcome to a new dawn of endless possibilities with many reasons to be cheerful."

He sent me that text at 5:30 a.m. I know because I archived the message. And shockingly, RDJ died of an unexpected heart attack later that same day.

I will never forget him and the impact he made on me—and so many others—through his words and his consistent actions.

We teach people how to treat us.

We only have a short time on this planet, dear ones, so why not make the most of it? How do you talk to yourself? How do you show up for others? It matters.

Why Disrupting Negative Self-Talk Is Essential for Your Growth

The importance of breaking free from negative self-talk goes beyond just feeling better about yourself. Research shows that shifting your internal dialogue can lead to real, measurable changes in your life. While psychologist and author Carol Dweck's work on growth mindset[3] is often referenced, there's more to the story.

A study published in the *Journal of Personality and Social Psychology* found that people who engage in positive self-talk are more resilient in the face of challenges. By reframing negative thoughts, they're more likely to persevere through setbacks and continue striving toward their goals. They don't see failure as a reflection of their character, but rather as a stepping stone for learning and improvement.

Another study from the American Psychological Association revealed that the language we use with ourselves shapes our emotional and physical responses. Participants who replaced negative self-talk with affirmations experienced lower stress levels, reduced anxiety, and improved overall well-being. It's not just about thinking happy thoughts—it's about rewiring your brain to support growth, resilience, and achievement.

Identifying Negative Self-Talk: What Words to Watch For

As I mentioned in my ADD principle, before we can disrupt negative self-talk, we need to become aware of it. This can be tricky, as many of these thoughts have become so automatic that they slip by unnoticed. In addition to the words you wrote down a moment ago when I asked you to consider how you describe yourself, I'd like you to read through this list of general red-flag words and phrases that my clients have shared with me. These are telltale signs of limiting beliefs:

- **"I always mess up."** This is an overgeneralization. We all make mistakes, but telling yourself that you *always* fail is simply untrue. It traps you in a cycle of defeatism.
- **"I'm not good enough."** This is one of the most common forms of negative self-talk. It's also too general and unspecific and a belief rooted in insecurity. I've found it often stems from a specific moment in childhood when we internalized someone else's opinion.

- **"I'll never be able to do that."** Words like never are absolute, and they leave no room for growth or possibility. They box you into a mindset of limitation.
- **"They're so much better than me."** Remember in Chapter 1, negative comparisons are a toxic habit that fuels negative self-talk. They shift your focus from your own progress to someone else's achievements, making it harder to celebrate your own growth.
- **"If only I were [smarter, faster, more extroverted]…"** Focusing on what you lack creates a scarcity mindset. It keeps you in a place of dissatisfaction and makes it difficult to appreciate your strengths.

The good news is, now that you know this, you can take more control. You can become more purposeful and mindful about communicating and connecting. You can start designing who you want to be. It starts with what you tell yourself. Your internal talk track directly correlates to your current level of self-awareness and self-confidence.

The first person you speak to in the morning and the last person you speak to at night is you.

Because we live so much of our lives in our heads, it's important to examine what we tell ourselves.

So, let's re-examine your descriptions list, the positive descriptions, and the not-so-good ones. Maybe they came from others, maybe they come from you. This time, divide the words into descriptions that support and encourage you and those that do not.

Descriptions that serve me	Descriptions that do not serve me
1.	1.
2.	2.
3.	3.
4.	4.
5.	5.
6.	6.
7.	7.

Change Your Actions, Change Your Thoughts

It's time to seriously interrogate the words and phrases we use to describe ourselves. Why are they in our minds, and who put them there? How valid are they really? We can redirect and modify the way we think about ourselves.

As I mentioned, I'm not a psychologist, but you might be recognizing this approach as part of the *growth mindset* concept first coined by a very impactful American psychologist, Carol Dweck.[4] More than thirty years ago, Dr. Dweck shared a powerful idea: we can change the way we think—just like we can improve a tennis serve or get better at playing piano. My piano teacher used to make me practice scales for hours. It wasn't always fun, but with every session, I improved. Sometimes just a little—but still, it was progress. And eventually, that improvement became my new normal.

That's what growth looks like.

Apply my ADD principle. Through increased awareness, you can identify your desires and goals and then get serious about the required discipline and practice it will take to achieve them.

First popularized by the incomparable author and speaker Simon Sinek,[5] many other authors, coaches, and leaders today spend a lot of time out there talking about the importance of finding your *why*. I agree it's important, but my next chapters are going to be less about finding your *why*, and more about helping you find and hone your *how*. This is because my clients tell me that they have been given feedback like, "You need to be more concise," or "You need to exude more authority," but the managers don't provide specific tools on how to go about making any of those changes my clients are being urged to make. This book gives you plenty of details on how to *amplify* yourself. Each tool becomes part of your new overall approach to *how* you connect with others and yourself.

Perception is reality until proven otherwise.

Those three SAP leaders who wanted to fine-tune their executive presence had to first understand how they perceived themselves and then how others perceived them. Now that you have a clearer understanding of your inner voice—where it came from, which words and phrases are helping you, and which ones might be holding you back—it's time to discover and apply my proven methods for replacing self-limiting thoughts with more powerful and positive words that will help you become the version of yourself you aspire to become. Your new and improved amplified self!

Yes, you will need to modify some of your default thoughts and behaviors. And sometimes, that triggers defensiveness.

The name of the game is to reframe.

Techniques to Disrupt Negative Self-Talk

So, how do we break free? Luckily, there are strategies to help you disrupt and reframe these unhelpful thoughts.

1. **Activate Your External Observer Mindset.** I want you to picture your thought patterns like a sled on a hill in the wintertime. If you sled down that hill numerous times, the path the sled takes begins to form a groove. After a while, no matter where you start that sled at the top of the hill, it will likely slide into the groove. It's the same with our neural pathways—the way we think. Our thought patterns are hard to break. So, we start with observation. Mindfulness is about becoming aware of your thoughts without judgment. Don't be a boat without an oar. You *can* take more control. Remember our letter "D" for discipline.

   Disrupting patterns or changing your current groove will take a conscious effort.

   The next time you notice one of your negative self-talk phrases creeping in, pause. Ask yourself, *Is this really true?* More often than not, you'll find that the answer is no.

   Activating your observer mindset will create a much-needed space between thought and reaction, allowing you to choose a different response.

2. **Challenge the Thought in Writing.** Once you've identified a negative thought, it's time to challenge it. Let's say you catch yourself thinking, *I'm terrible at giving presentations*. Instead of

accepting that as a fact, challenge the thought through action. I don't think it's good enough to stay in your thoughts by simply asking yourself, "What evidence do I have that this is true?" or "What evidence do I have that it's not true?" Instead, I suggest you grab a pen and paper and write out a list. The act of physically writing *by hand* is much stickier with the logical, rational, and organizational side of your mind than the more ephemeral and prone-to-wander emotional side of your brain.

Get out of your head and onto paper.

As you make a list of why this thought is or is not based in fact, you will probably recall you have successfully delivered a presentation in the past, or received positive feedback from peers when you spoke about a project or something perhaps less formal than a full-blown presentation. Even a small redirection can reduce the emotional negativity that accompanies our thoughts. Challenging the thought through writing helps you diminish its impact by putting it in a more balanced light.

3. **Create a Positive Counter-Statement.** For every negative thought, create a positive counter-statement that you can repeat to yourself. If your inner critic says, "You're not good enough," respond immediately with your new affirmation: "I am capable, and I'm learning every day." I'm going to encourage you to add your new affirmations *out loud* as an even more effective disrupter. Speaking positive affirmations aloud, while awkward at first, can help more quickly rewire your brain to focus on your strengths rather than your perceived weaknesses.
4. **Seek Out External Neutral Feedback.** If you're finding it hard to change your negative "groove talk" by yourself, get someone to help. Another way to combat negative self-talk is by seeking constructive feedback from a trusted colleague or mentor. Don't pick someone who will only tell you what they think you want to hear. Turn to someone who can provide a more objective perspective and help you see your strengths more clearly. Sometimes, all it takes is an external voice to remind you that you're doing better than you think.

5. **Substitute Negative Phrases with Believable, Empowering Ones.** While you're busy searching for new ways to disrupt or reframe your old negative thoughts, remember your new, positive statements must be *believable*. If your brain doesn't buy it, it won't stick, and you'll slide back into the old groove. Here are a few examples of how you can reframe common negative thoughts.

✓ **Negative Thought:** "I always mess up."
✓ **Reframe:** "I've made mistakes, but I've also learned from them. I'm improving every day."
✓ **Negative Thought:** "I'm not a leader."
✓ **Reframe:** "I'm developing my leadership skills. I have strengths that can inspire others."
✓ **Negative Thought:** "I'll never be as successful as them."
✓ **Reframe:** "Everyone's journey is different. I'm focusing on my own growth and progress."
✓ **Negative Thought:** "I'm not good at remembering names."
✓ **Reframe:** "I'm making a commitment to focus more on learning names."

The goal is to create statements that acknowledge where you are while also leaving room for growth. Instead of dismissing your abilities, reframing allows you to honor the progress you are making and the potential you have.

Our brains are remarkable in their ability to change. You may have read that neuroplasticity is the brain's capacity to form new neural connections, even as we age. I have seen the way people can grow firsthand and develop their abilities. Over time and with practice, they change the way they think about themselves. It's the same with you reading this right now. With consistent effort, you can literally rewire your brain to think differently.

Overcoming Imposter Syndrome

Like I felt when my first clients asked me to coach them on enhancing their executive presence, imposter syndrome occurs when a person doubts their abilities and feels like a fraud, even if they've achieved previous success or recognition. Unlike the pervasive negative self-talk we've already covered, something new and uncertain usually triggers this feeling.

For example, when you're faced with a new project, a new job, or a promotion. It's that unsettling voice in your head that tells you, "I don't belong here," or "I'm not good enough." It's incredibly common. Studies suggest that up to eighty percent of people worldwide say they have experienced it at some point.[6] Yes, that means nearly everyone—from entry-level employees to CEOs—have felt like an imposter, questioning whether they deserve their success or whether they're just lucky.

Knowing this can be a relief in itself because it highlights one of the most important truths about imposter syndrome: You're not alone.

That brings us to my top five tips for dealing with imposter syndrome:

1. **Remember You're Not Alone.** Just knowing that imposter syndrome is something many people experience—even those who are very successful—can help you feel less alone. It's a common mental pattern, not a sign that you're not good enough. It doesn't reflect your true abilities—it just *feels* like it does.
2. **Reframe the Thought.** As I've encouraged you to disrupt those old refrains that are floating around in your head and not serving you, the same goes when imposter syndrome creeps in. It's crucial to challenge and reframe the feeling. Instead of thinking, *I don't deserve to be here*, remind yourself, *I've earned my place. I'm a hard worker. I have gained skills before and I can do it again.* When you quickly strive to reframe negative self-talk into a more realistic, positive perspective, you can disrupt the mental spiral before it gains momentum.
3. **Push Through.** Sometimes, the best way to deal with imposter syndrome is to take action anyway. The more you step out of your comfort zone and succeed in new challenges, the more you chip away at those feelings of being an imposter.

Confidence often comes from doing, not thinking.

So, even when you don't feel entirely sure of yourself, push through and keep moving forward.

4. **Get a Coach.** Working with a coach can be invaluable in overcoming imposter syndrome. Coaches can help you gain clarity on your strengths, guide you through reframing negative thoughts, and offer accountability as you build confidence. A good coach will help you see yourself more objectively and remind you of your accomplishments, helping you break free from the grip of self-doubt.
5. **Journal.** Journaling is another powerful tool for battling imposter syndrome. Research shows that the simple act of writing by hand can help reduce the emotional intensity of anxious thoughts.[7] By putting your feelings down on paper, you create distance between yourself and your thoughts, which allows you to process them more rationally. Journaling also helps you track your progress and see how far you've come, which can be a helpful antidote to feeling like an imposter.

Reducing your moments of imposter syndrome, like reprogramming your baseline negative thought patterns, *is* achievable.

Engaging in positive self-talk and reframing exercises strengthens the neural pathways associated with optimism, resilience, and success. The more you practice, the easier it becomes for your brain to default to more empowering thoughts.

We can absolutely retrain our default behaviors, but it requires focus and effort. One of my favorite examples of moving from default to design occurred when I moved to Ireland from the United States and bought my first car. As an American, of course, I had spent my entire driving life on the right side of the road. So, my heart almost leapt into my throat when the dealer handed me the car keys, and I realized I would have to drive out of the dealership onto the left side of the road.

Everything I'd known as second nature, from hand placement on the steering wheel to spatial awareness, suddenly needed my full attention. Roundabouts, which the Irish are very fond of, became my greatest challenge. My instinct was to go in the opposite direction! The muscle memory that had guided me effortlessly for years wasn't reliable anymore. I had to think about every move, from staying in my lane to maneuvering through traffic circles without ending up on the wrong side.

At first, it was frustrating, even nerve-wracking. But I stayed committed, practicing mindful driving every time I got behind the wheel. Slowly but surely, I adjusted. My hands found a comfortable place on the steering wheel, and I safely sailed through those once-confusing roundabouts. Now, I'm proud to say I'm not only a safe driver but also the proud possessor of an Irish driver's license.

During the process, I needed to work past negative self-talk like, "You're too old to learn to drive in a new way." In the same way, I had to work diligently to overcome the once overwhelming and hurtful label of being a mumbler. What once felt like a limitation has become a driving force for continued growth. I no longer feel insecure; instead, I feel empowered by the progress I've made. Words others use don't need to define you—how you rise in response does.

Now, more than ever, with the increase in the use of virtual meetings, our voice is the calling card of our communications. How do you feel about yours?

Discover More About Self-Talk: How to Take Control of How You Talk to You

To remind you how you can take more control of your self-talk and how you talk in your mind about yourself, please scan this QR code. Next up, we'll explore how you can take more control of how you talk to others.

3

Tuning Your Voice Like a Pro

It's Not Just What You Say, It's How They Hear It

"The human voice is the most beautiful instrument of all, but it is the most difficult to play."

—Richard Strauss

Learn to Play Your Voice Like the Instrument It Is

"I HATE MY VOICE."

I get this complaint from people all over the world. Native English speakers and second-language English speakers alike. Many people express discomfort with how their voice sounds, and the reasons can vary, but here are some of the most common:

1. **"My Voice Sounds Different to Me."** One of the most surprising things people learn is that their voice sounds different when they hear it played back on a recording. This is because when we speak, we hear our voice through internal vibrations in our skull, which adds a deeper tone. When we hear a recording, we're only hearing the external sound, which tends to be a bit higher and lighter. Hearing it can be jarring to us and make us feel uncomfortable. I remember hearing myself the first time I laid down voice-over for a news story for CNN in the recording studio. The quiet of the room and the presence of the large microphone created a disconcerting effect for me. I felt out of my body somehow. I definitely didn't enjoy it.

2. **"My Voice Doesn't Match My Personality."** Some clients tell me they feel their voice doesn't match how they think about themselves or the persona they want to project. For example, a person who sees themselves as a strong leader might feel undermined if their voice sounds too soft, too high-pitched, or lacking in authority. (Keep reading, I promise you can refine this!)

3. **Self-Criticism.** Many people have internalized self-judgment and are too quick to criticize themselves. You might believe your voice sounds too nasal, too monotone, or too "annoying," even if no one else shares that opinion. Remember Chapter 2 and our discussion about negative self-talk? This is another application, folks. Take control and stop accepting your old way of thinking about yourself!

4. **Cultural Conditioning.** Some clients, particularly women, have felt pressure to speak more softly or politely, which can lead to vocal habits that undermine their authority, like ending statements with a questioning upward intonation or speaking in a quieter tone. Conversely, some men may feel pressure to sound more assertive, which could make them uncomfortable if their natural tone is gentler. I want to point out that I don't agree with the real or presumed pressures that still exist, which might make someone speak either of these ways. I'm just laying out the situations that some of my clients tell me they find themselves in.

Your voice has the power to inspire others.

Back Home Again in Indiana

To tell you about the first time I became aware of the quality of my own speaking voice requires us to revisit my hometown of Farmland, Indiana. I haven't described it in much detail up to now, so let me paint you a more vivid picture.

As you might imagine, it's a tiny town nestled in the rural Midwest of the United States, and yes, Farmland is really the proper name, not just a description of the area. With a population of just over a thousand, there are more cornfields, cows, and pigs than there are people. There isn't a stoplight. The tallest building when I was growing up was—and still is—the grain elevator.

My parents, along with my little sister, brother, and I, moved to Farmland when I was about seven years old from a larger town in northern Indiana, near the metropolis of Chicago, where there are many buildings higher than a grain elevator. My parents spoke more like city folk, but because I was very young when we moved there, I grew up speaking like my new friends and neighbors. I spoke with a thick country accent.

For example, one of my favorite teachers was Mrs. Washler. But I didn't pronounce it how you might be imagining this if you were reading her last name right now. I pronounced it like my friends did: Mrs. *Worsh*ler.

In the same way, we didn't wash our clothes in Farmland, Indiana. We *worshed* our clothes. I am not making fun of this accent or dialect of American English—I'm simply describing the way we talked.

By the time I had reached about ten years old, I was beginning to dream of becoming a journalist. When I read stories in the newspapers or watched reports from far-off places like Paris, London, or Cairo, I envisioned myself traveling there. I wanted to tell people's stories and report from the exotic places where those headlines were made.

So, imagine the jolt I received when we made a visit to Chicagoland to visit my mom's friend, Sharon. She owned a hair salon and my mother took us to get our haircuts there for cheap when we would go to visit our grandparents and other family members who lived in the area. Sharon was trimming my hair and chatting with my mom and me when she commented to my mother, "You know, Gina really sounds like the cutest little country girl. She's like someone out of Huck Finn." My mom said, "I know. She should have a little stalk of wheat in her mouth."

This conversation wasn't a blow to my self-confidence the way the Mumbles remark had been a couple of years before. Maybe because I was a bit older and learned how to take it. Also, I loved Sharon. She was like a cool auntie I looked up to. Her observation, then, served more like a wake-up call.

If I wanted to realize my dream of not only being a print reporter, but ultimately becoming a television journalist reporting live from the White House, how well would my current accent serve me?

Imagine listening to me as I pronounced our nation's capital city during a live, on-air report with the same accent I used to describe my favorite teacher. I would pronounce Washington as *Worsh*ington. I resolved to do better.

You don't have to change everything to make meaningful progress in how you speak. You are in control.

You can make deliberate choices about what parts of your current style you want to keep, and what speaking patterns you would like to evolve.

Communicating to Be Better Understood

I eventually went off to college and, while studying journalism and political science, I also worked at softening my accent. But I want to stress that while I endeavored to develop my ability to communicate clearly and effectively, I also began making some conscious choices about some of the small-town core values I learned growing up that I wanted to keep with me.

For example, I learned that taking baked goods or a fresh-from-the-oven casserole to someone who is hurting is a good thing. This gesture became very poignant for me when my dad died unexpectedly in a plane crash when I was eleven years old.

It wasn't a large commercial plane. Dad was the pilot of a small plane for a small company. He was flying alone back to his home hangar after dropping the company's president off at a nearby town. It was two weeks before Christmas, and there was heavy fog that December night. As Dad was coming in for a landing, he somehow clipped trees about 500 yards from the runway. We'll never know for sure why it happened, only the tragic outcome. While my family struggled to come to grips with everything, the community surrounded us with an outpouring of kindness and casseroles. Mom didn't need to cook for weeks.

Be Kind While You Are Able

Of course, it wasn't so much about the food as it was the company. Some people talked. Some people just sat with us. The deep loss changed me forever. I learned at a young age that life is fragile and uncertain. That's one of the driving reasons it's so massively important to demonstrate as much care and compassion as you can while you're still able. None of us know how much time we have left. I hope you embrace the notion that time is precious, and we don't want to waste a single minute. **So, let's commit to taking control of what we can while we can.**

I am convinced that compassionate communication can be developed and grown alongside any other positive trait and characteristic you want as a more amplified version of you. Often it takes effort to slow down, stop, and listen.

I share this with you to let you know that I didn't just pop out fully formed. It took, and it still takes, desire, determination, hard work, and ongoing efforts like the ones I'm now inviting you to make.

You can simultaneously be proud of where you come from and excited about where you're heading.

I am proud of the caring values I experienced while my family grieved and later, as I grew up in Farmland. I'm also proud that I remain connected with so many friends I made during my time there. However, when I went away to college, I am also proud that I decided to dedicate myself to modifying the way I enunciated a couple of words and softening my overall accent in order to be better understood.

Let's Elucidate Why It's Helpful to Enunciate

I can promise you that I now consistently pronounce *Wash*ington like it reads, and not *Worsh*ington, like I once did. My evolved, developed, or changed pronunciation certainly served me better than my previous pronunciation would have when I was delivering all those live reports in front of the White House during my time as a news correspondent.

More recently, the more neutral diction I now use regularly when I speak also serves me well when I'm delivering keynote addresses or leading training sessions around the world. From Greece to Saudi Arabia, Bulgaria, Ghana—no matter where I go, I want everyone to be able to easily understand me. The way I pronounce words matters. Same for you.

A few years ago, after a speaking engagement in the charming Mediterranean town of Sidi Bou Said, Tunisia, I was seated with some of the local attendees and another American presenter. I'll call him Chuck.

"Why was it so much easier to understand what Gina was saying than when you spoke, Chuck?" asked a bold woman who had been in the audience during the day's conference.

"Well, I do tend to speak pretty fast," Chuck began.

"No, it's more than that. I couldn't understand a lot of your words—even when you were speaking slowly."

"I know why," another lady chimed in. "Gina speaks more clearly and distinctly."

I promise I'm not making up this conversation, and I'm not trying to brag or throw poor Chuck under the bus. I'm trying to make the point that making an effort to control your voice makes a difference in how much you will connect with your audience. Just an example of why all this matters.

No matter your background, your career, or your family situation, you can benefit by learning to say what you say a little better. When someone says, "I don't want to be fake." I say, "You won't be." You should be proud of where you're from, just like I am. Being proud of who you are today and having an intention to grow and change are not mutually exclusive.

Your self-acceptance and your self-development can live in harmony.

So, let's get started on your own enunciation, shall we? Here's a practical exercise to get you going. **Make a list of five to ten words** that you either know are difficult to pronounce or that others have pointed out to you as being unclear. If you're a native English speaker, you might drop the "G" in words like "running," "walking," or "going." Instead, you say, "runnin," "walkin," or "goin." Or perhaps you slur words together too quickly, turning "did you" into "didja," or "what are you" into "whatcha." While this may not pose an issue when speaking with close friends, it can be problematic when you're addressing an audience, especially if they include speakers who have English as a second language.

If you're a non-native speaker reading this book, the words you focus on will be different. I want to stress that I am not urging you to completely eliminate your accent. It's a reflection of who you are and where you come from. For instance, I have lived in Ireland now for nearly ten years, and while I do try to enunciate my words, I still speak with an American accent. It would likely sound contrived if I forced myself into speaking with an Irish accent. In fact, the first year I was here, I did try to slide in the word "grand" that the Irish regularly use instead of "fine" into a casual greeting exchange, and it went like this:

I was in the check-out line at a grocery store in the Irish city of Cork when the local cashier at the register glanced up at me.

"How're you doing today?" she asked, probably without really thinking. It was simply the routine way she greeted countless customers at her conveyor belt.

"Ah, sure, I'm *grand*," I replied, thinking how well I was assimilating into my new Irish culture by using that word. She stopped and looked at me again, more closely this time. Detecting my American accent, she now realized that I wasn't Irish even though I had borrowed their oft-used adjective.

"No." She decreed, "It doesn't suit you."

That settled it. I would need to revert to responding with "fine" or "great, thanks." Something more in keeping with my country of origin.

For the record, the incident with the grocery clerk was amusing. She was gently poking fun at my efforts—the Irish would call this *slagging*. And it is funny, isn't it? Communication is a constant give and take. A recalibration. A balancing act of situational awareness. On the one hand, yes, you want to show interest and awareness and curiosity about the culture you may find yourself in, but you also need to be genuine to your core.

Your accent is part of your identity, and I encourage you to embrace it. However, if your accent is particularly thick, there may be certain words or sounds that could use some refining to ensure your audience can follow along easily.

Here's a grid to help you organize words and phrases you may want to modify.

Words I Would Like to Pronounce More Clearly

The word or phrase	How I sound	How I would like to sound
1.		
2.		
3.		
4.		
5.		

My friend—actor, screenwriter, and co-writer of business books, Dave Pliler—helped me organize a lot of my thoughts for this book. He asked, "How can you help people take more control of their voice through a book?" I recognize I can't hear the changes you will try to make. But as I've said before, when you write things down, it helps you focus and prioritize, so please take a moment to start the list and even write the phonetic way you are pronouncing the word and how you would like to pronounce it. After you've made your list of tricky words, it's time to try my "Isolate and Integrate" technique:

1. **Isolate.** Take each word from your list and pronounce it in an exaggerated way, really focusing on each sound. Repeat the word five times in isolation, being as clear as possible.
2. **Integrate.** Now, take that word and use it in a sentence. Repeat the sentence five times, still focusing on clear pronunciation.

Here's an example. A few weeks ago, at the time of writing, one of my clients, who is a native French speaker, was preparing to speak on a panel put together by *The Guardian,* a newspaper based in the United Kingdom. Rehearsing his thanks to the organizers, I noticed he pronounced the paper's name as *The Gwardian*, giving the letter U a W sound, rather than keeping it silent.

I asked him to repeat the correct pronunciation of the name five times slowly and clearly. That's the *isolating* exercise.

"Gar-dee-an
Gar-dee-an
Gar-dee-an
Gar-dee-an
Gar-dee-an"

Then I asked him to incorporate that single word with its upgraded pronunciation into the actual thank-you sentence he planned to say during his panel appearance. He rehearsed that line out loud five times: "I especially want to make sure and thank our organizer for today's event, *The Gar-dee-an*." He repeated that aloud five times. That's the *incorporating* portion of the exercise.

Now, select one of your words and then insert it into a sentence. Practice this technique five times for five days and watch how much more fluid and understandable you will become in just a short amount of time. Don't forget: both exercises must be spoken **out loud**.

Record Your Vocal Baseline

Remember, we'll have another QR code at the end of this chapter where you can click and experience me giving audible examples of all the techniques I'm describing to you in writing. I want to encourage you to think about your voice as an instrument that you can learn to play purposefully, just like the trumpet or the violin. You wouldn't think of playing in a recital or taking to the stage without first practicing your instrument, so why do so many people expect their voices to perform well without daily purposeful practice?

You don't rise to the level of the performance, you fall to the level of your (aloud) practice.

Before I present a few more important elements of your voice that you can take more control of, grab your phone and voice-record yourself reading something right now to capture your vocal baseline. This is a separate awareness-building exercise from your keyword enunciation exploration that we just covered.

Read anything aloud: a cereal box, a paragraph from some marketing material in your workplace, or anything from a book or a magazine article you're reading. Whatever. Make it short, about twenty to thirty seconds will do it. Next, listen to the recording. I don't want you to worry about what you look like because we'll talk about that later. For our purposes here, I just want you to heighten your awareness, to begin to understand what you are doing—or not doing—with your voice when you read.

Okay, put your phone down. That's enough for now. Well done. You've made a great start.

At the end of the chapter, I'll ask you to record yourself reading that same selection again. I want you to compare the two. This is how you can practice, explore, and track your vocal progression.

Your voice is an instrument. Learn how to play it!

Practicing silently in your head is simply not the same, so make sure you vocalize these exercises.

Listen Up and Enunciate

Scan the QR code and watch me demonstrate what to listen for when you record yourself reading a passage on your phone. I'll teach you to be your own voice coach.

Projection: Speaking with Purpose and Presence

Once you've begun to work on diction and enunciation at your current baseline level of conversation, the next layer to add is **projection**. Projection is often misunderstood. It's not about yelling or raising your voice to an uncomfortable level; rather, it's about speaking with enough volume and presence to fill the room or reach every easily distracted ear in a virtual audience.

Think of it as **pushing your voice to the back wall** of the room. This naturally adds volume but doesn't necessarily increase intensity or aggression. The goal is to project your voice outward with purpose. By doing this, you'll also find that you automatically start to *slow down* as you project, which further aids in clarity.

Remember, if your audience has to strain to hear you, they'll lose interest or disengage quickly. Practicing projection is crucial, especially in virtual meetings where technology can sometimes muffle your voice. It's the number one sense you can use to connect with your audience in a virtual setting. A well-projected voice will help you maintain a strong presence, even through a screen across thousands of miles.

Of course, there are times when speaking quietly is a strategic advantage. If you want to have people feel you are sharing a secret in confidence, you might lower your voice, even around a boardroom or meeting table, to give them your personal reflections.

However, in most group settings, projection will help you obtain and maintain your space or your speaking floor. I once had a client who spoke so softly that her colleagues and manager constantly asked her to repeat herself. When her first performance review came back, her supervisors gave her good marks for meeting her deadlines, but they reached out to me to help her learn how to *amplify* her voice so she would instill confidence in the people she was required to meet.

When I first met her, I learned she came from a family culture where children were taught to be seen and not heard. She had grown up being encouraged not to speak much louder than a whisper. She equated volume or projection with sounding harsh. "I don't want to sound mean. I don't want to sound like I'm trying to boss people around," she said with concern. But anyone can learn to project their voice and over time, with practice and plenty of encouragement from me, she did.

As with my client, the great news is that when you project your voice, if you also infuse your voice with upbeat energy and enthusiasm, you will not sound mean or severe.

Make Projection Progress

Want to hear me demonstrate what I mean when I say, "projection?"

Scan this QR code and I'll show you.

Phrasing and Fullness: The Chocolate River

Being able to be heard is the first part of getting your point across, but projecting your voice also adds roundness to it that will help people not only hear you, but *want to listen* to you. When you layer roundness into your voice on top of your newfound volume, it creates a more soothing and listenable experience, which is different from pure volume for volume's sake.

The image I would like you to imagine is a dark, warm chocolate river. It's flowing, like a hot fudge sundae, or one of those chocolate fountains at a wedding that you can put a strawberry or a marshmallow in. I went to a wedding once that had one, and convinced myself it was healthy because I dipped strawberries in it.

Anyway, the idea here is that the flow of your voice, the smoothness of each word as you attach it to the next one, should be like the *legato* phrasing in a musical composition. Legato is an Italian word used in musical notation, which means tied together or linked in a smooth way.

Your vocal projection combined with roundness will be more listenable. Another way to add roundness is to imagine you are slightly stretching or extending your vowels in words that you want to emphasize. Here is an example:

"Thank you so much to the editors of *The Guaarr-dian* for inviting me here tonight."

This is not about stretching so much you sound like a Shakespearean actor, but just a little elongation to make a point. If you are speaking about something important and you elongate the vowels, it will actually stretch the experience for the listener's ear and engage them in a different way than if you purposely just made your consonants crisp. When you project your voice and combine crisp consonants with rounder vowels to create words and phrasing that flow like a smooth, warm, chocolate river, you are creating a voice that is a sweet delight to listen to. Certainly, one that is more enjoyable to listen to than someone who has not given any of this a second thought.

Reaching Round and Resonant Tones

Yes, I've had clients tell me the idea of rounding vowels or sharpening consonants sounds confusing, forced, and unnecessary.

Scan the QR code here and I'll give you a short lesson on how to swim the chocolate river.

Pacing and the Power of the Pause

When you're presenting, pacing is one of the most important tools to keep your audience engaged and drive your message home. Whether you're delivering a business proposal, giving a keynote, or leading a team meeting, knowing when to slow down and when to pick up the pace can make all the difference in how your message is received. The key is to develop control over your pacing, which requires practice, awareness, and intention.

Slowing Down Adds Gravitas

There are moments when slowing down is essential. It can emphasize the importance of what you're saying and give your words weight. Think about delivering a key insight, a powerful statement, or a call to action for your employees or teammates. If you rush through it, you risk it going unnoticed. Unremembered. Unactioned. But by deliberately slowing your speech, you allow the audience time to digest, reflect, and be impacted by your words. I like to encourage my clients to end their important points "low and slow," combining lower pitch with a gradually slowing pace.

Slowing down gives you an air of authority. It shows that you're confident and in control of the room. When you're speaking more slowly, it gives the impression that you think your ideas are worth listening to. People naturally associate slower, deliberate speech with someone who is composed, thoughtful, and authoritative.

Speeding Up Adds Energy

On the other hand, pacing doesn't always mean you should speak slowly. When you're sharing an exciting or upbeat story, or when you're trying to build energy in the room, it's natural to speed up. A faster pace can create a sense of urgency, excitement, and momentum. Your audience will feel that energy and will stay on the edge of their seats as they anticipate what's next.

The key is to strike a balance. If you're always talking too fast, you can overwhelm or confuse your listeners. But if you vary your speed, speaking more quickly when you're excited and slowing down for important moments, you're taking your audience on a dynamic journey. Study any Sunday morning church pastor worth listening to and you will see examples of varied pacing.

Nervousness Leads to Rushing

Too much speed and you may veer out of control. Your mouth doesn't keep up with your mind. This happens a lot when people are extremely nervous. It's completely natural to want to rush through a presentation when you're uncomfortable. *Just get this over with, right?* The problem is that when we speed up due to nerves, we lose control of the pacing, and the audience can easily lose track of what we're saying.

This is where my love of rehearsal comes into play again. Practicing aloud helps you identify the moments when you naturally tend to speed up. By recording yourself or rehearsing in front of someone else, you can learn where to take control and consciously slow down. Try practicing speaking even slower than normal. This can feel awkward at first, but it helps train your brain to resist the urge to rush.

Pausing with Purpose

Pauses are incredibly powerful. They give your audience time to process information and keep your speech from feeling cluttered. Strategic pauses also help eliminate those distracting filler words—*um, uh, you know*—which can weaken your impact as a speaker.

One way to practice the power of pausing is to take a deep breath before beginning each sentence or important point. It helps calm your nerves and prevents the rush of words from spilling out too quickly. Another exercise is to mark intentional pauses in your speech or script, like a conductor would mark up an orchestral composition. Pausing allows you to feel more in control and gives the people in your audience time to absorb what you're saying.

Two Exercises to Practice Pacing Control

1. **The "Slow It Down" Drill.** Take a short section of your presentation and deliver it *much* slower than you normally would. Draw out each word in an exaggerated manner. Like you're walking through mud. Pay attention to how each word feels and how your pauses create space for impact. This will help you build an awareness of where slowing down can add authority to your speech.

2. **Pause-and-Breathe**. As you practice your presentation, insert a pause every time you would normally say "uh" or "um." Instead of filling space with a filler word, take a deep breath and let the pause do the work. This will help you learn how to replace nervous fillers with confident silences.

Playing with Pacing and Pausing

When you click the QR code, I'll deliver a few sentences in a number of ways so you can hear for yourself what it means to use the power of the pause to reduce fillers and keep your listener with you when you speak.

The Ups and Downs of Your Pitch

When we're speaking, the word *pitch* refers to the highness or lowness of tone as perceived by the listeners' ears. You may have an idea of your natural pitch, but don't forget your voice sounds different depending on whether you're listening from inside or outside of your head. Pitch is often used in a higher range to denote enthusiasm or energy and lower when we're talking about something serious, or something that we want to make sure has a sense of urgency.

Others are forced to listen to us, so we should, too.

To help you learn more about the range of your natural pitch, grab something and record yourself for another thirty seconds. When you play it back, listen for pitch—in addition to enunciation and projection. Do you speak in a range that is so high it is hard to understand? Is it so low that you sound muffled, or mumbling? Try reading and recording the selection again, this time intentionally stepping up or down just a degree or two while still feeling comfortable.

What you're aiming for is to explore your natural range. And since most of us have not determined or defined where our everyday voice lands, getting comfortable recording yourself is so helpful. When you land on a level that you like, keep reading. Go for about two minutes at the same pitch. Two minutes a day will start to give you a different baseline pitch level over time, one that you can replicate and default to easily.

I once had a client who was a junior partner in a prominent law firm tell me that a senior partner had told her, "Since you're a woman, you need to speak with a lower voice to be taken more seriously." That advice frustrated her because she felt it was unfairly aimed at her just because she was a woman. The register of anyone's voice can, and should, be better explored in order to amplify you and your message. Try recording yourself reading a paragraph at a few different pitch levels within your own natural range. Play it back for someone you trust and ask their opinion. Then make a decision if you'd like to move your normal speaking voice up or down even half a step. It's doable.

The Ups and Downs of Pitch

If you're not sure how to begin to explore playing with pitch, scan this handy QR code and I'll talk you through it. Literally.

Inflection Is Infectious

Let's talk about inflection—how your voice rises, falls, and adds emphasis. Inflection helps highlight what's important in a sentence. It might be just one word, or a short phrase, but the key is this: not everything should sound the same. Speaking in a flat, monotone way loses your listener. Instead, match your voice to the meaning of your words. If something sounds exciting, urgent, or emotional, your voice should reflect that—maybe with more volume or energy. Or if something's meant to feel intimate, soften your voice and lower your volume. Try it out as you read—experiment with which words you choose to emphasize and how it changes the feeling.

Don't get hung up on landing on the perfect version. There isn't one. The first time I had to track a script for a report—before my CNN days—I was working for a local news channel in Washington, DC. As I rehearsed my script aloud walking into the recording booth, I remember being frustrated that it felt like there were too many ways I could interpret the read-through.

If I decided to emphasize *this* word, then the story felt *this* way. But if I decided to inflect a different word, then it felt a different way. So, I read it in a variety of different ways until I ultimately recorded the one that seemed to fit the emotion of the story best.

There are still a variety of ways to add interest, depending on the words you choose to emphasize:

Fresh Fish Sold Here Today.

Try reading the above line aloud five times. Each time, have fun punching or emphasizing a different word.

Fresh Fish Sold Here Today.
Fresh **Fish** Sold Here Today.
Fresh Fish **Sold** Here Today.
Fresh Fish Sold **Here** Today.
Fresh Fish Sold Here **Today**.

Imagine the audience's experience as you read each line. Which one would you finally settle on? If I were going to read it, I think mine would be something like this:

Fresh *Fish* Sold Here **Today**.

There is, of course, no perfect way to read this line. But the point is to learn to explore, make a choice, and back up your choice with intentionality.

The trouble with most business presentations and other forms of professional communication, like team updates or financial projections, is that the words are too evenly spoken, resulting in white noise that is just way too easy to tune out. So, let's tune you up!

Accentuating Emphasis

Most of us have never even tried playing around with emphasis when we present, but here's your opportunity. Click the QR code, and let's try it together.

Vibrant Voices

Let's talk about energy and passion. In business settings, just as with everyday life, vocal energy matters. There is a hope and a dream or a fear attached to even the most seemingly ordinary or banal sales report or quarterly projections.

The more we can learn to deliberately bring energy to our voice, the more we will demonstrate to our audience that we care and are connected to the emotions propelling the words. Even if you are required to repeat similar reports, you can infuse energy into your voice *every* time.

The energy in a leader's voice sets the mood for the whole meeting.

A regional vice-president coaching client from a large multinational tech company asked me to help him with what he described as his "canned corporate speeches."

"I'm so tired of them," he complained. "I've said some of these phrases thousands of times, and I'm so bored."

I said, "It might be the thousandth time for you, but it's likely the first time for your audience. If you sound bored, how can your audience believe you or take to heart even one word of what you're saying?"

For him to successfully do right by his message, he needs to turn on the energy in his voice. Notice I say, "He needs to." There are very few exceptions to this from where I sit. It's your responsibility to role-model behavior as a leader. Bringing vocal energy is a requirement for leaders—or anyone hoping to become a leader—in the workplace.

Exuding vocal energy often comes from speaking at a quicker pace, with more projection, and enthusiastic and interested facial features (we'll tackle body language in Chapter 4, so keep reading). Most people have a low-energy expectation for routine meetings—and even conferences—because that is the way most of them are delivered.

"Ho-hum, here comes the weekly sales, finance, operations, marketing, insert-your-department-here update, yippee." Does that sound familiar?

You can do better. Even if you use the same words but infuse more energy into your tone, you're mixing up the status quo, and that changes the way people experience you, the topic, and the meeting in general. Now, I'm not suggesting that you go out and buy cheerleader pom-poms, but I am asking you to dial yourself up if you are prone to monotone.

We all have different versions of ourselves. There is human magic in learning how to dial ourselves up or down, depending on the situation.

You can dial yourself up or down.

Go back to that cereal box. Even if you're just reading out ingredients about wheat, rice, or barley, imagine it will change the health of the person who eats it every morning.

Bring the Energy

Bringing energy is different than simply projecting your voice. But the two techniques are connected.

Scan the QR code here and I'll show you how to habit-stack for success.

Wake Up to the Power of Words

We've covered the importance of energy and passion, of inflection and emphasis, of variety, of pitch, of pace, and the power of your projection. I now want to remind you of the power of words. You've heard this plenty before, but it's worth repeating:

Words matter.

Words create worlds.

If you are speaking jargon that you know because you're an expert in an industry, but you are speaking to brand new hires or perhaps a college roadshow, and you haven't simplified those words, you may have left your audience behind. No one cares how smart you sound if they miss the message.

Most new hires or junior employees won't feel confident to stop you and ask you to explain a technical term you casually uttered, or provide the fuller meaning for some fancy acronym the company casually uses to describe a complicated process or particular department. They're left trying to swim in the bowl of alphabet soup you just delivered. Have you become so accustomed to the business-speak in your company or industry that you've forgotten how to talk like a regular human?

Consider this real example from a real company: **"We're using commercially sustainable business models to drive transformative acceleration."**

Why not just say, **"We're changing the way we work to get better results."** Or even infuse more energy into your everyday words like: **"It's time to change things up here at [XYZ] company! And I'm excited to tell you about all the great results we're going to achieve together."**

Even if you have a great-sounding voice, if you don't choose your words carefully, you won't connect as well as you could to the other humans in the room. If you must refer to something with its acronym or technical term, add a layman's-level descriptor right afterward to keep everyone—not only the insiders—with you as you speak.

A university professor once proudly proclaimed to me, "Only two other people I know understand my dissertation."

Hmmm, I thought to myself, *How is that a good thing?*

It's not all about dumbing it down, which is a phrase I don't like, for obvious reasons. Instead, choosing to include more layman's language becomes an equalizer—a humanizer. That should be our goal.

My approach to achieving this in my writing and my speaking, when I'm asked to deliver a workshop or a keynote, can be discovered behind a funny quote that is often misattributed to Ernest Hemingway. Turns out he never said it, but I can still imagine the rough and salty writer saying:

Write drunk.
Edit sober. 😉

Of course, I'm not seriously advising you to pop over to your local pub and get yourself hammered before you draft your next report. But I do want you to freely toss everything out there. Brain-dump your ideas, and don't worry if you've used jargon or clunky wording. After you have completed your draft, read through it *aloud* (which I did for everything you're reading). Look for words you can warm up, power up, and simplify.

We often write differently than we speak, so it's essential to read your copy aloud to test whether it even sounds like you. Or anybody. If it doesn't, make a change. And hey, this is where you could use ChatGPT to your human advantage. Put your questionable phrases or paragraphs into the application's prompt and ask it to "provide a more conversational version." Then, you can read what it spits out and make your decision from there. You're still the human being in the room who needs to speak the words, but now you can use tech tools to help you.

When you speak with words that are more inclusive, positive, imaginative, or inspirational, you are setting yourself apart as a more positive, imaginative, and inspirational leader.

The Wonder of Words

If you'd like to hear me provide some examples of where you can power up or warm up your words, give this code a scan.

As I mentioned to you, this girl from Farmland, Indiana, has taken more control over her voice, but I've not denied or abandoned my cultural background or the story of how and where I grew up. It takes time and effort, but taking control of your impact by learning to play your voice like an instrument and choosing your words more carefully and intentionally will not make you disingenuous. I promise. With good intentions, the more positive and purposeful version of you will impact others around you in a more positive way.

You don't have to settle for the same voice you have used for the past ten, twenty, thirty, or more years. You're focusing on your lasting legacy and impact. Each of us can begin to take more control of our voice.

Since our voice comes from our mouth and our mouth happens to live on our face, it's now time to focus on the second section of this book: our body language. Now that we agree we can learn to take more control of our innermost thoughts and learn to play our voice more actively like the instrument it is, we must also take more responsibility to match our sound with how we look.

Putting It All Together

Learning to really play your voice like the instrument it is takes time. Here I recap everything in this chapter to remind you of what we've covered so you can maximize your impact.

PART 2 Look It!

4 Facing the Finesse of First Impressions

Seen Before Heard

"You never get a second chance to make a first impression."

—Will Rogers

You Are Extraordinary

GIVE YOURSELF A ROUND OF APPLAUSE.

Before we dive into Part II and explore how to take more control of our body language and appearance to impact ourselves and others more positively, I first want to say, "You are extraordinary."

A couple of years ago, I was interviewing renowned executive coach and best-selling author Marshall Goldsmith for the weekly business and leadership column I write in Ireland's largest circulated newspaper, *The Sunday Independent*.[1] I asked him about his latest book and his advice for ordinary people. "I don't write for ordinary people," he flatly responded. "Ordinary people don't read books," he explained. "And when they do, they don't get past Chapter 3." So, welcome to Chapter 4 and to being extraordinary.

As I mentioned in the opening chapters, my ADD principle is the foundation which we build upon to become more purposeful connectors and communicators.

Awareness.

Desire.

Discipline.

When you keep combining these three together, you're unstoppable. View them as your three drivers of personal mastery.

1. **Awareness.** You must first *see* where you are, understand what you need to improve, and recognize your strengths and weaknesses. Without awareness, there is no starting point.
2. **Desire.** Once you're aware, you need the internal *drive* to take action. Desire is the fuel that propels you forward toward your goals, transforming what you know into what you *want* to achieve.
3. **Discipline.** Finally, to turn that desire into reality, you need consistent *action*. Discipline is the sustained effort, the structure, and the commitment that ensures long-term success. It keeps you on track even when motivation wanes.

Together, these principles form a powerful trio. Without awareness, desire is aimless. Without desire, discipline feels empty. And without discipline, awareness and desire remain just ideas. These three work in harmony to create lasting change and personal mastery.

Speaking of harmony, let's recap. So far, we've covered the notion that your self-acceptance and self-development should also live in harmony. I've stressed that professional improvement is not a competitive endeavor. It's uniquely personal to you. We examined your self-talk, along with its roots and causes, and discussed ways to disrupt the thoughts that no longer serve you well. We unpacked and repacked with purpose several vocal variety techniques you can use to take more control in order to better connect with your fellow humans.

One by one, we are exploring and examining a characteristic, approach, trait, strategy, or other form of a developable tool that you can choose to apply to amplify yourself. You've likely heard the term "habit stacking,"[2] first coined in 2018 when James Clear wrote his bestselling book,

Atomic Habits. But the fundamental idea has been around for a long time. Being committed to lifelong learning and growth, I am convinced that we can unpack and repack, with more intention and purpose, each of the simultaneously interacting gears that turn whenever we have a communications event. And don't forget, *everything* is a communications event.

Now, let's stack a new awareness and commitment onto our stack of building blocks—to continue to improve the way we connect with others, and ourselves.

I'm talking about intentional *body language*.

Everyone's an expert at reading body language, but few of us are experts at delivering it.

⋆ ⋆ ⋆

I'm in Lagos, standing at the front of an expansive training room in Nigerian Breweries, a subsidiary of Heineken. The room fans upward from where I stand. It's an auditorium-style, elevated arrangement of classroom seating. Normally, the rooms I lead training sessions in are company boardrooms or off-site conference rooms, which keep me standing at the same level that the gathered participants are sitting. But not today. About thirty senior leaders are peering down at me from their seats, waiting for our session on executive presence to begin. It's a bit intimidating, like I'm looking upward at a team of courtroom judges. I scan the room. Thankfully, most of the participants are gazing back down at me with smiling, pleasant faces. All but one. There she is. The woman seated in the first row to my far left. Her eyes are narrowed. Her lips are pulled into a scowl. She tilts her head down onto her notebook and writes something.

Oh wow, I think. *What did she just write? What's going on with her? She really looks like she doesn't want to be here.*

Her face has made me uncertain—a bit nervous. But the show must go on. I introduce myself to the assembled group and kick off our training session. I glance back over to who I will now secretly call "Miss Grouchy," or "Miss G" for short. She is still at it. Her expression is so tight she looks like she's just bitten into an unusually sour lemon and is blaming it on me.

I launch into our first group activity and invite everyone to come out of their seats and join me down at the center of the room for a leadership collaboration exercise. I divide the group into four teams. Miss G joins in with her group. At this point, I find myself surprised to see how much effort and positive energy she appears to be putting into the exercise. She's smiling and laughing and fully engaging with her peers. When we're finished, I ask everyone to return to their seats and I seek a volunteer to reflect on what has transpired.

I'm even more surprised now because Miss G is the first person to raise her hand. Now smiling broadly, she enthusiastically describes her team's approach and outlines some terrific takeaways. The discussion continues with others chiming in, but I can't stop thinking about Miss G. Her sour face at the beginning hasn't synced with her energetic participation. I need to sort this out. During our first coffee break, I walk over to her.

"Hi there, may I talk with you for a moment?" I ask.

"Sure. I'm loving your session so far," she says, smiling again. "I'm getting so much out of everything."

"That's exactly what I want to explore with you," I begin. We have moved away from the other participants, who are now busying themselves with refreshments, so I hope it's a perfect opportunity for a private chat. "When I arrived and first looked out at you this morning, your face looked to me like you were unhappy, even possibly hostile to the idea of taking part in today's session. I was genuinely worried."

"Oh my gosh," Miss G exclaimed. "I had no idea. Are you telling me I have 'resting b★tch face'?"

We both laughed at her choosing to use that colorful description for how her listening or at rest face appeared. You've likely heard it before yourself. I hope it wasn't regarding you. But back to Miss G. While I stopped short of repeating the term she used, I confirmed that, yes, her scowling face had indeed sent me a message of, at best, disinterest and, at worst, absolute irritation. She assured me she was unaware of this and that it was unintentional.

And this, folks, is where we begin. Remember, we are *never not communicating*. My dear Miss G was emitting negative signals to me—and likely many others around her over the past months or even years—regardless of whether she meant to.

The Importance of Body Language

Body language matters because our communication is about more than just words. And yet, in my experience in professional settings all around the world, body language is one of the most important, yet often overlooked, aspects of leadership communication.

Whether we are in a one-on-one conversation, delivering a presentation, or simply entering a room, we are constantly sending signals to those around us, even when we're not speaking. These nonverbal cues, intentional or not, shape how others perceive us—our confidence, interest, enthusiasm, or authority.

One common misconception is that people are judging us based on how we look, as if it's purely superficial. But it's not about looks—it's about understanding the signals we're broadcasting. We humans are wired to make sense of our environment and simplify complex social interactions. We instinctively interpret the signals we receive from body language to assess someone's intentions, mood, or engagement. This is not a judgment of physical appearance, but rather an assessment of behavior.

Like I was with Miss G in Lagos, our minds are constantly trying to answer questions about the other people we're interacting with: *Is this person confident? Are they paying attention? Are they genuinely interested in what I am saying?*

Our brains are bombarded with countless stimuli every second. In any interaction, environmental distractions, external noise, and our own internal thoughts compete for attention. In fact, research shows that as our smartphone use increases, our attention spans are decreasing, making it even harder for us to fully engage. As a result, we simplify our surroundings by making quick assumptions based on the body language we observe. It's largely an automatic process—part of our brain's way of conserving energy by reducing the amount of information it has to process. It's easier to make a quick judgment about someone based on their posture, facial expressions, or gestures than it is to overanalyze the context of the situation.

Because these judgments happen so quickly, it is essential that we are mindful of the signals we send. Take the example of someone slouching in a meeting. It may seem harmless, but the message it sends to others could be one of disinterest or a lack of confidence, even if that's not how they feel.

On the flip side, a person who sits upright, makes steady eye contact, and uses open, welcoming gestures projects confidence and authority—again, without saying a word.

What makes this even more crucial is what I keep repeating: We are always communicating, even when we think we're not. Avoiding eye contact, sneaking a peek at our phone, or looking off into the distance, all send negative signals. You might believe you're appearing neutral or even relaxed, but others may perceive it as closed off or disengaged. Your expression doesn't only impact the speaker, it also impacts the other people who may be seated around you.

Imagine that you're a student in a school assembly. A teacher is talking, and you notice a cool kid who looks annoyed. If you're highly impressionable, you may be inclined to copy the look on the other student's face. Soon, the annoyed look triggers a chain reaction, spreading from one student to the next, transforming the mood of the room and ensuring that the teacher's lesson won't get taught.

The Domino Effect of Disinterest

I recently witnessed the same thing during a professional All-Hands meeting. Employees from each department across the country were gathered in a ballroom for an off-site monthly update. I was standing to the side. The managing director had asked me to make some observations about the cohesion of his senior leadership team, who had taken up seats in a row at the front. When the HR director came up to begin her presentation, I noticed the chief operating officer immediately looked down at her watch. She then slouched back into her chair as an expression of boredom swept across her face. Within seconds, I noticed that other operations team members seemed to be imitating what they were picking up from their department head.

It was like watching a virus spread, visibly. Contagious. Nearly everyone on the operations team changed their expressions and looked more checked out than they had appeared just moments before when the managing director was speaking. By the way, let me assure you, sharp readers, that the HR leader was not a super-boring presenter. She spoke in a similar manner to that of the previous presenter. I was convinced the junior team members were taking cues they were observing from their leader.

This wasn't the first time, of course. The managing director had been noticing it for some time, but he wanted a third party to validate his suspicion and, if confirmed, he wanted me to address the issue with her. Later, in private, I discussed everything with the operations director. Like Miss G, she claimed that she had no idea she was sending off negative vibes.

The Three Cs of Body Language

Your body language is always at work, conveying messages about who you are, how you feel, and what you're thinking, whether or not you're aware of it.

Given that people naturally interpret our body language as part of their effort to make sense of their environment, we must take control of these nonverbal cues. It's about ensuring that our body language aligns with our intentions, so others aren't making incorrect assumptions about us. When we understand the power of body language, we can use it as a tool to communicate more effectively, build stronger connections, and convey the right message at the right time.

We read each other in three main ways:

1. **Context.** The environment in which you are communicating shapes how your body language is received. Your face should match the setting—whether it's a professional presentation or a casual conversation over coffee.
2. **Clusters.** Body language doesn't happen in isolation. It's a combination of gestures, facial expressions, and posture that collectively form a message. For example, a warm smile paired with direct eye contact and an open posture signals trustworthiness.
3. **Consistency.** The congruence between your words and your facial expressions must be in sync. If you're delivering good news but your face remains neutral or tense, your audience will feel confused or even distrustful.

While body language varies slightly across cultures, the fundamentals are remarkably similar, especially when it comes to the face. Regardless of where you are in the world, certain facial expressions convey universal emotions: a smile denotes warmth, raised eyebrows signal surprise, and narrowed eyes often indicate displeasure.

Do our facial expressions align with what we're saying? Understanding how to manage and project positive body language through the face is vital to creating trust, rapport, and effective communication.

The Face: Our First Point of Contact

Just as it was when I glanced up at Miss G, imagine you're meeting someone for the first time. Whether it's in-person or virtual, the moment they enter the room or the camera comes on, the first thing you notice is how that person looks, isn't it? (And I'm not talking about clothing, hairstyle, or accessories here, although I will cover all that in Chapter 6.) I'm talking about the way they are reaching into themselves to demonstrate that you, as the other person in their view, or who is a part of their audience, are worthy of their attention. We have the power to signal that the other person is valued or is worthy of our time simply by the way we choose to emanate that worth through our face.

In person and on virtual platforms, the face is the first thing people notice. From the tilt of our head to the set of our jaw, we're constantly giving cues. So how can we ensure that we're sending the right signals?

Your Mouth: A Powerful Messenger

Our mouth does more than just speak; it reflects emotions even when we're silent. A genuine smile is one of the strongest signals of positivity and warmth. It doesn't always come naturally to many of us.

Take "Jack," a regional leader in healthcare I once coached. Jack had received feedback that his neutral face was perceived as severe, although I wouldn't have used that word myself. However, his big, tall stature, combined with his large physicality, deep-set eyes, heavy eyebrows, and strong nose definitely was imposing. He conveyed a sense of presence and stature that commanded attention, but without layering on a smile, which he rarely did, I could imagine how he could seem severe or menacing to a junior employee.

Remember, I'm not here to pass judgment on the features we were born with, but it is fair to say that some features work together for us to read "approachable" or "pleasant," while others combine to read "intense" or "serious." As with any aspect of self-development, it's essential that we understand our baseline so we can adjust and be more accessible.

Jack asked me how he could exude a more welcoming presence. I asked him to smile. The smile he produced was one with his lips still pressed tightly together. No wonder his colleagues interpreted even that as disapproving. Jack wasn't unhappy with anyone, but he was unaware of the impression this expression was sending.

I helped him reprogram his muscles by practicing a softer, more relaxed smile with a slightly open mouth. Within a few weeks, he noticed a shift in how people interacted with him. His neutral face became less intimidating, allowing him to build stronger relationships at work.

At the other end of the spectrum, a smile that's overly wide and shows every tooth can come across as fake. As an American, I'm especially aware of the stereotype—it's that overly eager, always grinning character from old TV shows and movies. You know the one: the used car salesman in the loud suit, always smiling too much and selling with a bit too much enthusiasm. It's a caricature, of course, but it's also a reminder that when a smile feels forced or constant, it can feel insincere. I was reminded of this during my very first training trip.

I was a volunteer trainer with the nonprofit organization Freedom House. My mission was to provide support to television journalists in Romania, which had just overthrown forty years of communism and state-run media. I had spent the last three days showing up to my assignment destination: the newsroom of a brand-new independent television station. I was smiling and shaking hands and introducing myself to as many of the journalists as I could in order to build attendance for my upcoming newsgathering training session.

On the third day, the station's top female news presenter, who had noticed me trying to work the room over the previous days, walked up to me.

"You Americans smile so much," she began, "I think you all must have gas."

Ouch. Maybe she had a point. Perhaps I had been guilty of overdoing my smile. Each of us can become more situationally aware.

All this fuss about a smile?

You might be thinking as you read this. Yes. In my experience, the littlest of changes can make a big difference. I don't want you to suffer paralysis by analysis, but I do want to encourage you to pay attention to the details about yourself that you are communicating to others.

Smiling is one of the most powerful tools we have to connect with others and regulate our own emotions. It sends a nonverbal message of warmth, reassurance, and approachability. Studies show that soft smiling fosters trust and openness between people, making it easier to establish rapport and break down social barriers. But beyond its external effects, smiling also has an internal benefit—helping us reduce tension and shift our mood, even when the smile doesn't initially feel genuine.

The neuroscience benefits for us behind smiling are also fascinating. Research indicates that when we smile, the facial muscles involved trigger a neural response that activates the release of neurotransmitters like dopamine, serotonin, and endorphins—the body's natural feel-good chemicals. This reaction can lower our stress levels, calm the body, and enhance our overall sense of well-being. Even the simple act of smiling when we're stressed can produce these positive effects, effectively relaxing the body and mind, which in turn makes it easier to face the challenges in front of us.

Perhaps most interesting is the notion that we can benefit from smiling even when we don't particularly feel like it. Known as the facial feedback hypothesis, this idea suggests that facial expressions can influence our emotional state. In other words, by smiling—especially when we're feeling tense or down—we can actually improve our mood. This is not to say that we should suppress negative emotions or fake happiness, but intentionally smiling does help guide our mindset toward a more positive outlook. Smiling is, in this sense, a proactive way to shift our emotional state.

Imagine yourself in a situation where you might be prone to feeling anxious or disconnected—perhaps in a tense meeting, or during a difficult conversation. Choosing to smile, even slightly, can help bridge that gap, allowing you to feel more at ease and communicate that you are more open to others. It doesn't matter if the initial smile feels forced or unnatural. Over time, the act of smiling can become more relaxed and genuine, as the body naturally begins to reflect the emotional state that the smile helps create. It's like a self-fulfilling prophecy.

One common misconception about smiling in this way is that it feels inauthentic, or like we're faking it. However, it's important to distinguish between suppressing feelings and choosing to manage them in a healthy way. Smiling isn't about denying stress or negativity. Instead, it's about shifting focus to others and making a conscious choice to engage in a positive, constructive manner. When we smile, we're not pretending that everything is perfect; rather, we're signaling to others that we care about how they feel and are willing to offer warmth and kindness.

Smiling Is a Choice

Like every facet of becoming a more purposeful and intentional human connector, smiling is a choice that allows us to connect with others while also benefiting ourselves. By focusing on the positive impact our smile can have on those around us, we're able to adjust our mindset to become more others-focused. This, in turn, reduces our own tension and helps us feel more grounded. Far from being a superficial act, smiling is a powerful way to manage both our internal and external worlds, creating a cycle of positivity that benefits everyone involved.

By the way, I'm happy to report that the anchorwoman in the Romanian newsroom, who first commented on my overdone smile, has gone on to become one of my dearest friends. It's been more than twenty years since that original conversation, which she swears she has no recollection of, and I love Anca like a sister. In fact, she is the godmother of my daughter, Lulu.

The Eyes: The Windows to Your Message

Your eyes also speak beyond words. When we make deliberate, active eye contact, we signal to others that we are present, interested, and genuinely paying attention. It's more than just looking at someone—it's about connecting, and showing that you value their words and perspective. Eye contact demonstrates confidence and credibility, while also making the other person feel seen and heard. It's a silent but powerful way of saying, "You matter to me in this moment."

Whether in a one-on-one conversation, presenting to a group, or sitting in an audience, providing proper eye contact is essential. But in the same way as I've discussed raising your awareness and application around smiling, you must learn how to strike a balance when it comes to your gaze. Too much intensity and you risk coming across as aggressive. Too little, and you may appear disinterested or detached in the same way I experienced Miss G in Lagos.

A good visualization technique to deploy when it comes to thinking about smiling with your eyes is to imagine you are projecting soft eyes, much like my notion of transmitting a soft smile. Softening your gaze means that you are telling yourself to remember to be fully present while you are speaking and/or listening. You are looking with interest. Become aware of the shape of your eyes and eyebrows together. Often, when showing interest, we may raise our eyebrows a bit. If the topic is serious, we may furrow our eyebrows in solidarity with the urgency of the topic. Most of us do this naturally when we are in emotional conversations with people we are very close to. But if you turn this active eye energy off when you are in meetings or interviews or other business professional networking situations, you are turning off an additional mechanism to indicate your intended connection with other humans.

When it comes to presentations, look at the eyes of the other people in the room. A client of mine from a large telecom company once told me that she had been coached to "look right above the audience's faces"—apparently so she wouldn't get nervous. But I wholly disagree with that. Instead, make an effort to connect with people by gently scanning the room and briefly locking eyes with different members of the audience. As you speak, allow your face to reflect the emotion behind your words. If you're discussing something urgent, your face should show that urgency. When speaking about something more compassionate, soften your expression.

When people see that you see them—in a positive way, of course—they will often increase their engagement with you as a result because they literally and figuratively understand that they are being seen.

In virtual meetings, eye contact becomes more nuanced. It's easy to look at yourself on the screen or drift off while others are speaking. As much as possible, train yourself to look into the camera when addressing other people or when you are in the listening position. This simulates real-life eye contact.

Beyond just maintaining eye contact in that virtual setting, remember it's crucial to ensure your eyes are engaged—meaning they are animated, expressive, and match the emotional tone of the conversation. Engaged eyes enhance your message and reinforce your connection with the other person.

In social and professional settings, mastering the art of eye contact allows you to build stronger relationships, create trust, and show respect. Our eyes are a key tool in our body-language toolkit that helps others feel valued, while reinforcing a positive, lasting impression of you!

The Tilt of the Head: Subtle Yet Impactful

I can't let this chapter wrap up before I spend a moment reminding you that even the way you tilt your head sends messages about your engagement level.

When someone is speaking and you're listening, a slight tilt can signal curiosity or empathy, while a rigid, straight head might suggest disinterest. When it comes to the virtual world and presentations on the various platforms there, I can tell you from personal experience that a little head movement definitely helps a speaker feel like they're not monologuing to a bunch of cardboard cutouts. When your camera is on and your mute button is pressed, if you are just sitting there with no expression or head movement, it can really deflate a speaker's enthusiasm.

When someone is speaking, occasionally demonstrate understanding or empathy with the content through a nod or gentle head tilt. This shows that you're actively listening and encourages the speaker to continue.

Framing the Head in Virtual Spaces

Since I've already mentioned virtual platforms, let's take a moment here to explore the new frontier of new challenges for body language.

When you're on a video call, the framing of your face matters. As soon as the camera comes on, people make a quick judgment on how you're coming through on that screen. For the optimal and most pleasing shot, aim for your face and torso to be in the center of the frame. Give yourself a little headroom from the top of your head, but not too much. If you show up with too much, you risk looking like a puppet head bobbing on the lower edge of the screen. Too little headspace probably makes you appear cramped, with your head coming too close to the camera, which is uncomfortable for the person on the other end of the video call. Position yourself with a comfortable amount of space around your head, ensuring your facial expressions are fully visible.

Make sure your Zoom room has even lighting, too. If you are lit from one side, it can create an eclipse across your face. If you're standing in front of windows, I suggest you close the curtains or blinds, so the natural light behind you doesn't make your face come through the screen in silhouette.

If we can't see your face, we can't read the crucial body language coming from your face at all. And, of course, that's no good.

The Power of Active Listening

Engaging your mouth, activating your eyes, and being mindful of how you move your head while speaking or listening isn't performative or faking it—it's about heightening your awareness and taking responsibility for how you communicate. These are natural tools nature gave us to signal connection, understanding, and care to others. When we focus on these aspects of body language, we're not pretending or masking our true selves. Instead, we are intentionally using the abilities we already have to strengthen our interactions.

Our facial expressions, eye contact, and head movements are all integral parts of how humans have evolved to connect with one another. When you consciously engage these tools, you're showing that you're invested in the moment and in the other person. This creates an environment where trust and connection can flourish.

Far from being an artificial performance, this is all part of the series of choices you can make to demonstrate that you are more thoughtful and deliberate in your human interactions. By focusing on these cues, you demonstrate that you care enough to communicate clearly, which helps others feel valued and understood. It's about making the most of the natural signals we send as humans, then using those to build stronger, more authentic connections.

Practical Steps to Improve Facial Communication

1. **Practice with a Mirror.** This might feel awkward at first, but it's an excellent way to see how your default facial expressions come across.
2. **Ask for Feedback.** If you're unsure about your resting face, ask someone you trust for their honest opinion.
3. **Record Yourself.** In virtual meetings, record yourself and see how your expressions align with your message.
4. **Be Mindful of Context.** Adjust your facial expressions depending on the setting and the topic.

Remember, your face is the front line of your communication arsenal. Whether you're speaking to one person or a thousand, how you use it will determine whether your message connects. The choice is up to you. You can own this and take more control. Or you can dismiss it as unnecessary or fake.

Unfortunately, I'm sorry to say that the operations director became defensive when I shared my observations of her during that townhall meeting. (Don't forget that her director had already witnessed this behavior a number of times and was concerned about how her behavior was impacting her relationships with the other department heads and rippling out to negatively impact the rest of her team.)

"I am listening even if my face doesn't look like I am," she complained.

Of course, but the point is that she isn't living in solitary confinement. Her facial expression sent messages to others around her.

On the other, happy side of the choice coin, I can share that when Miss G (I still think of her as Miss G—but now the "G" stands for glowing, not grouchy) and I finished our private feedback meeting, she committed to taking more active control of how she chose to hold her mouth and eyes when she was in a more passive listening mode.

From the time she returned to her seat until the end of our training session, she looked back at me and the others gathered in that room with an actively engaged face. She didn't smile broadly like a clown, but pressed her lips together in a slight, upward curve, creating a soft, "Mona Lisa" smile.

To accompany the expression, she also occasionally nodded lightly or cocked her head. The overall experience was that of an aware, active listener seeking to engage, connect, and support the speaker. She confided in me during our afternoon break that she was even enjoying herself more.

"I find that by activating my face, I not only send purposeful positivity to the speaker, but I have become more focused on the content myself, as a result," she said. "I'm retaining more."

I was so pleased. Job well done.

Another body-language signal Miss G deployed, as I looked up at her in the auditorium that day after our talk, was to lean forward into her chair about thirty degrees, another clear sign of interest. Beyond our face, we have much more in our body-language arsenal that we can activate.

What Is Your Face Saying?

Join me for a look at how we look when we look. When you click the QR code, I will go through some of the elements I've covered around how to improve your facial expressions to better connect with others.

5 From Fidget to Focus

Taming Unintentional Movements

"I like to move it, move it.
You like to move it, move it. Move it."

—King Julian from the film *Madagascar*
(originally recorded by Reel 2 Real)

Change Your Actions, Change Your Thoughts

I WAS PREPARING TO DELIVER THE SCARIEST SPEECH OF MY LIFE.

Wait. I didn't say what I meant. It wasn't the speech that was scary. It was simply that I was feeling scared. Nervous. Anxious. And this was strange, because I happened to be in one of the most calm-inducing places one could imagine. Picture me standing in a charming room in a quaint B&B on the scenic Isle of Wight near the south coast of England in 2022.

I should have been relaxed. But I was not. I was rehearsing the TEDx talk I was to deliver in just a couple of hours and I was feeling overwhelmed.

As someone who regularly coaches executives on public speaking, you'd think I would have been cool as the proverbial cucumber, right? Not at all. TEDx talks aren't your average, off-the-cuff presentations. They are timed to the second—literally. If you run over eighteen minutes, your talk won't make it to TED's holy grail of YouTube uploads. I was feeling enormous pressure to make sure my speech was perfect.

The title of my talk was "The Myth of Authenticity," and while the topic is clearly something I care deeply about, no amount of passion could erase the fact that this talk had to be memorized, word for word. Not to mention my slides had to fit TED's particular visual aesthetic. You get the idea. There was no room for improvisation, no casual banter with the crowd. Every second had to be accounted for.

Months before, when I had written my initial script, I hired a TED coach to review my draft and help me punch it up. (Thank you again, Julie Burstein![1]) But now it was up to me to deliver it. I couldn't wing it. So even before breakfast on the day of the event, there I was in front of the mirror in my room, running the script for the umpteenth time.

I was to be the final, featured speaker, which of course added extra intensity to the day.

By the time I arrived backstage to be miked up, nine presenters had already gone before me, and I could feel the collective energy in the room starting to dip. My internal monologue was something along the lines of, "Okay, Gina, you need to bring them back to life. You're their last speaker—don't let them fall asleep on your watch!"

The audience was full, and when my name was called, I walked onto the stage feeling a sense of detachment. It was like I was watching myself from outside my body—something I've only experienced a handful of times.

But here's the great news: every word landed perfectly; the jokes hit at all the right moments, and the audience laughed and clapped at the right places just like I had hoped they would. As I walked offstage, I mentally high-fived myself. I had really nailed it.

That's precisely when the floor director came up to me with a smile that didn't quite reach his eyes (and you know why we need to see a person's mouth and eyes in sync from reading the previous chapter).

"That was great," he said as he greeted me and then he added more slowly, "but there's one problem."

Oh no "One problem?" That doesn't sound good.

"Your earring kept hitting your headset mic. The audio is unusable for TED standards," he explained. Then he said exactly what I was afraid was going to come next:

You're going to have to do it again.

I stared at him, waiting for a possible punchline. But there was none. He wasn't kidding. My heart sank to my shoes. I wanted to cry. After all that work, all that effort, I had no other choice. I was going to have to deliver the entire talk again—but this time, the audience would have already gone home.

After about thirty minutes, back onto the stage I went. Now to perform for an empty theater. Thankfully, it was not entirely empty. A handful of the other speakers had kindly agreed to stay behind to cheer me on, clapping as enthusiastically as a group of six possibly could.

With no crowd energy to feed off, I had to dig deep.

I am not bragging here. It was a real challenge. But I managed to re-deliver every line, every gesture, every joke with as much intention and precision as before. It was an exercise in discipline and focus—mirroring exactly what I'm excited to be sharing with you in this chapter: *the impact of intentional posture, gesture, and movement.*

So, dear readers, remember this: how you move and hold yourself is a developable human skill like any technical skill you train yourself to learn. Learning best practices and having more control over your body can help you add impact when presenting before a meeting room full of people or in a nearly empty theater.

Movement Requires Muscle Memory

Learning how to carry ourselves, whether standing, sitting, presenting in person, or even presenting virtually, is one of the most powerful tools we have for communication and improving human connections. Have you ever asked yourself any of the following questions?

- How do I walk into a room?
- How do I stand on the stage when I present?
- Should I pace across the room?
- What do I do when there's a podium?
- Do I stand or sit when I speak at a meeting around a table?
- How do I sit when I'm a participant speaking as part of a panel?
- What do I do with my hands?

My clients ask me these questions all the time. When you feel more confident and comfortable about these things, then you don't have to worry about them. Any nerves and anxiety will be reduced, and you can dedicate more brain focus to the content and material you've prepared.

Let's start with standing.

Stand Tall

Our posture can convey confidence, presence, and engagement—long before we even open our mouths to speak. When standing, think of your posture as your foundation.

You want to stand tall, with your head held high, as if a string is gently pulling from the crown of your head. Don't tip your chin up into the air or jut it too far forward, or you could come across as haughty, arrogant, or aloof. I recommend keeping your chin directly in front of you, or when you go to introduce yourself to someone or listen to someone speak, dip it ever so slightly down, while directing your gaze toward the other person.

Your shoulders should be slightly back, your core engaged, and your pelvis also can tilt forward just a little for balance and for a leaner look. This posture not only makes you appear more self-assured, but helps you feel more grounded.

You might be wondering, does all this attention to small details really matter?

The answer is yes—it does. When you take control of things like body language and how you physically carry yourself, they become second nature. That way, when you're presenting, you don't have to think about them—you can focus fully on what you're saying and how your audience is reacting.

"Paolo" was a middle-aged man and team leader of a large accountancy firm who, when I first met him, had a tendency to stand with his shoulders slouched and rolled forward. As with many of us, he wasn't even aware that this was how he held himself.

"I've never even thought about it," he responded when I asked him to describe to me how he stands. No surprise then that when he was required to walk to the front of a room to give client updates for the quarter, or take to the stage to present at a country-wide event, his body language spoke louder than his words.

Standing there, in a shoulder-slump slouch, he also shifted his weight from one leg to the other, making it hard for his audience to stay focused on what he was saying. His discomfort was obvious, and it affected the way others received his message.

We worked together to address this. I encouraged him to take more purposeful control of his posture—planting his feet evenly, standing with his weight balanced, and keeping his shoulders back. The change was immediate. **Not only did Paolo feel more confident, but his audience picked up on it as well.**

He later told me that team members had commented on how much stronger and more grounded he seemed. By making these simple adjustments, Paolo was able to connect with his audience better and convey his messages more clearly and with a more memorable impact.

Unless it's a very informal meeting with a small group of people all seated around a smallish table, I recommend standing during presentations. And even then, if you are the team leader or facilitator of the meeting, consider at least standing at the beginning to welcome everyone and set the expectations for the meeting. It can make for a nicer, more structured start.

As with the expansiveness of your smile and the intensity of your gaze, when it comes to developing or accentuating your standing posture, it's also important to remember cultural nuances in business settings. For example, in many Western business environments, standing tall with a firm stance exudes confidence and authority. While in some Asian cultures, choosing to exhibit a modest, restrained posture may be interpreted as more respectful. Being aware of these situational differences can enhance your connection with diverse audiences.

Don't Hide Behind the Podium

When it comes to those ubiquitous podiums that are placed on many presentation stages, avoid hiding behind them if possible.

I understand and appreciate that for many of you, especially if you are just beginning your public-speaking presentation journey, a podium can be a comfort zone. But it also becomes a barrier between you and your audience. Instead, stand to one side or step forward. Be near the center of the room or front of the stage whenever possible—just not too close, I don't want you falling off.

Once you're standing away from the podium, if you must use notes, try putting your content on an easier-to-manage iPad or tablet. You don't want to be seen shuffling around even the smallest of notecards or, worse yet, wrestling with full-sized pages of paper. This would necessitate you placing them on the podium to keep them from fluttering around in your hands. Practice holding the tablet in one hand and gesturing to the audience with your free hand. (I'll cover more about hands and gesturing in just a moment, so hang on.)

This combination of tablet plus free hand (to gesture) will only work if you are wearing either a lapel microphone or a headset—or, of course, if you're not using a microphone at all. If you are given a hand-held microphone, then you won't be able to use your free hand to swipe your tablet to advance your speech on the screen unless you time yourself to stop talking while you swipe.

I've seen this before. The speaker keeps speaking while they swipe up with the hand that is holding the microphone—and for a few seconds, no one can hear what they're saying anymore because they've moved the microphone away from their mouth. It's not the smooth audience experience we are aiming for. If you absolutely need to use the podium to place your notes in front of you, do it. But don't grab either side of the lectern and keep them glued there immobile. You will need to compensate for the barrier you've created by using your hands and making sure you look up and out toward your audience as much as possible.

Proximity matters.

Proximity is a powerful tool in public speaking, and its impact on engagement can't be overstated. I worked with a client, I will call her "Kersten," who had a habit of clenching the podium tightly during her presentations. She would stay rooted behind it, reading her notes with her head bent down, never making eye contact with the audience. Her connection to the people in the room was nearly non-existent, as she hid behind the lectern, both physically and metaphorically.

When I finally convinced Kersten to step out from behind the podium, moving to the center and front of the stage, everything changed. She stood exposed before her audience, vulnerable but present, and the energy shifted. By standing in the open, Kersten made eye contact and moved with intention. She felt the difference and, more importantly, so did her audience—they became more engaged and responsive simply because she was willing to meet them where they were.

This approach reminded me of another experience when I had the privilege of interviewing Bill Ford, Jr., the executive chairman of Ford, for a national event. We sat together on stage in two leather armchairs as I asked him to share stories from his childhood and experiences at the helm of one of the most influential companies in the world. His body language was very engaged as he sat (more on the topic of how to exude an executive presence even when you're seated in just a moment). For now, I want to focus here on his standing presence. Later that same evening, at a formal gala dinner event, I watched him choose to walk to the center of the room, not carrying any notes with him, stand still surrounded by tables, and speak for fifteen minutes about the importance and purpose of this gathering. His proximity and openness made him appear approachable, warm, and open, even at his level of leadership. It didn't diminish his authority; quite the opposite.

Of course, this wasn't an accident—he had trained and developed this style over time. Just like Kersten, anyone can learn how to master proximity to enhance their presence on stage. Choosing to stand in a manner that brings you physically closer to your audience helps create a sense of connection and engagement. The closer you are, the more real and present you will feel to them.

You can decide now who you want to be—what you want to be known for.

Walk This Way

When walking, stride with purpose—steady and comfortable. It should not feel like you're marching stiffly through a military drill, nor should you appear to saunter or drag your feet. The best practice globally, in my experience, is to move with intent, signaling that you're fully present and in control. This is especially true during presentations, where your posture can either distract or enhance the message you're conveying.

"Barry," the country director of a large food science organization, initially shuffled onto the stage during our rehearsal for an upcoming regional conference. This wasn't just any event—it was a major gathering of not only all his company's employees but also a wide range of clients and prospects. He was tasked with being the first speaker, the emcee, and facilitator, who would set the tone for the entire conference.

When I saw Barry's slow, hesitant entrance, I had to be direct but kind. "Barry," I said, "as the first person addressing this crowd, you have both the opportunity and the responsibility to establish the energy of this event. If you shuffle out there, what message are you sending about how much you care and the excitement of this event?" The answer was clear—his tentative entrance was setting a low bar for enthusiasm and engagement.

Now, because Barry isn't the type to start his presentation by doing jumping jacks or jogging onto the stage, I would never suggest such things. Instead, we worked on speeding up his walk just slightly, to give it more purpose. We also focused on how he could actively bring with him onto the stage a winning smile, as I described in the previous chapter.

In addition, I encouraged him to secretly, but intentionally, tighten his core once he completed his walk, to help him stand tall and continue to exude that stronger, more energetic presence. The result? He emanated a sense of excitement and professionalism before even uttering a single word.

Audiences need to feel like the time they're spending with you is valuable, and your body language can deliver that message long before you speak. Barry learned that every movement can either affirm or deny the value of the experience—and it's up to you to make sure you're affirming it.

Don't Be a Duck in a Shooting Gallery

Okay, you've walked with purpose onto the stage. You're not behind the podium, you are toward the front and center. And you have begun speaking. Now what?

One common mistake people make when presenting is pacing. Before you get frustrated and think, *But I must move around on the stage*, I'm not saying you should never move, just be very aware.

I think pacing falls into the advanced category. It can be effective for seasoned speakers, but for many, it manifests more as nervous energy than purposeful movement. The result if done wrong? You end up looking like a duck in a shooting gallery. I'm sure you've seen them up there on a stage at some time yourself. As soon as the ducks reach one side of the stage, they immediately turn around and dart back to the other side. Back and forth they go with such speed that you start forgetting to listen to what they're saying because you're too busy watching them zip from side to side.

Pacing can distract from your message.

Instead of pacing, I suggest anchoring yourself. Plant your feet about shoulder width apart and stay put. Keep your knees a bit soft, not locked. When they're locked, you might become unbalanced, or you might start bobbing by occasionally lifting your heels off the floor. Don't do that. It makes you look nervous, amateurish, and uncertain. You may be, but there is no need to signal that to your audience by bouncing or rocking.

If you want to move a bit, imagine one foot as the fixed leg of a math compass—step the other foot forward for emphasis when making a point while your fixed foot stays in place, then return the extended foot to rejoin your fixed position. This subtle movement adds energy without creating a clutter of unnecessary movement. When you decide to move to another part of the stage or room, do so deliberately. Once you've moved, stay there for a while, rather than constantly bouncing around. Too much movement scatters your audience's attention.

You Can Even Stand in Your Zoom Room

Let's not forget our hybrid working world and virtual settings. When you're presenting in a Zoom room (or Teams, or whatever platform you prefer), I encourage my clients to stand if they can. Standing brings a different energy—literally and figuratively—to your presence. I always stand during virtual meetings. Even when I'm traveling, I have created makeshift standing desks by stacking my suitcase and a few pillows onto the hotel desk and placing my laptop on top. The audience can't see my setup, but they see me come through the screen with more presence and energy than if I were slouched in a chair. It's a simple way to stay engaged and give your audience your best.

How to Take a Seat Like a Pro

Now, let's consider your posture when you're sitting. Whether in an interview, a meeting, or as a moderator or panelist, how you sit also influences how others perceive you.

The common mistake is to scoot all the way back in the chair, which invariably results in your body slouching or leaning back. I'm sure most people who do this are not giving it a thought, or are perhaps aiming to give off an air of relaxation, but it creates a look that appears sloppy or indifferent. When you sit in a very relaxed way, it can also relax your mind and attention span, so you mentally drift off. If you are seated in a panel in front of an audience, and you sit back and relax, this often makes you look heavier in the midsection, as your torso collapses like an accordion.

Instead, position yourself forward, toward the edge of your seat. This keeps your body active and engaged, rather than passive and slumped. For meetings or interviews, leaning in at about a thirty-degree angle conveys engagement and interest without looking overeager. But don't lean too far forward—it can look like you're ready to jump from your chair and bolt for the door! Moderation is key here.

If you're on a panel or speaking alongside slides, you'll also want to be mindful of how your body is positioned. For both men and women, I encourage you to not cross your legs. If your body is forward enough, put both feet on the floor. Women should have their knees together, one foot slightly in front of the other. This creates a clean line from your head to your toes and prevents the distracting nervous tendency I've seen too many times to bounce your suspended foot when your legs are crossed. Men can have their knees slightly apart, but should not do the man-spread.

Angle your body not only toward the other panelists and the moderator, but also your audience. Always be mindful of them, as you are presenting to *them*, not to your slides or fellow panelists. You can start by positioning your body in the direction of the moderator or other speakers, but make sure to turn physically and mentally toward the audience as you share your stories or insights.

When you're seated on a stage, you do not become invisible when you are not speaking.

And remember—when you're seated as part of a panel discussion, you don't disappear when you've finished speaking. You're still in front of that audience, and they're still watching you. I'm always surprised (but not shocked) when I watch a panelist who has either not yet spoken or has just completed their comment, appearing unaware that others are still watching them. Without notice, they drop their posture. The body collapses. Then their face appears to lose interest. I've even seen some who, like that operations director from earlier in the book, visibly check their watch or—gasp—even pick up their phone while they are *still sitting there on the stage.* Pay attention. Don't let this be you! Remember, we're always communicating, folks. Keep your face and body actively engaged at all times. When you're sitting quietly on a panel, even if you're not doing anything as crazy as checking your phone, if you lapse into passive body language, it will make you fade into the background at best or, at worst, appear rude toward the other guests.

In any setting—standing, sitting, or virtual—posture is key to executive presence. It's about more than just how you look; it's how you communicate your attentiveness, engagement, and professionalism. The way you carry yourself is a powerful signal to others that you care about what you're saying and doing—and you care about *them*. When you own your posture, you're not faking anything. You're simply taking control of the tools nature gave you to signal to others you're connected, present, and ready to engage. Whether standing tall on stage, sitting on the edge of your chair in a meeting, or standing in your Zoom room, the posture you choose will either enhance or detract from your message.

So, next time you're preparing to speak—whether to an audience of hundreds, a small meeting room, or even on a Zoom call—take a moment to think about how you're holding yourself. Because how you *stand, sit, and move* is just as powerful as the words you speak.

Using Gestures for Impact

"Marwa," the financial director of a prominent tech company in Egypt, had an impressive command of her data. Her insights were sharp, her strategies clear, and her work ethic impeccable. But whenever she presented to her team or the larger company, something was noticeably off. She would stand at the podium or at the front of the room, arms rigidly down at her sides, never moving them once throughout her *entire* presentation.

"I don't know what to do with my hands," she confessed to me in one of our coaching sessions. "And then, I'm so focused on what I've prepared to say that I just forget they're even there."

While Marwa delivered well-thought-out points verbally, the audience wasn't as engaged as they should have been because of her holistic disconnect. Her team was distracted by what I jokingly described to her as "frozen arm syndrome." When a speaker holds their arms stiffly at their sides, it creates a sense of discomfort for the audience. We're all sitting there waiting for something to happen that never does. The lack of movement draws attention away from the message and onto the speaker's posture, making the audience count the minutes until they finally raise their arms for some sort of gesture. Imagine how it feels to your audience if, like my wonderful client Marwa, you never raise your arms.

As a presenter, the goal is to have your message heard, not to make your audience fixate on the way you're standing. Marwa's case isn't uncommon. Many speakers struggle with what to do with their hands, often overcompensating by keeping them still or letting them flutter without control. I worked with Marwa to help her loosen up and recognize how intentional gestures can significantly impact her delivery.

What's the Best Resting Position

While there is nothing inherently wrong with starting a presentation with your hands down at your sides, it's important to know this shouldn't be your default for the entire talk. First, simply envision the distance to go from point A to point B. When your hands hang at your sides, it takes longer for them to travel up when you want to make a gesture. Additionally, leaving your arms stationary for too long can make you appear stiff or uncomfortable, and that's exactly how your audience will feel.

We human beings naturally move our hands when we are talking informally with friends and family. This is true across all cultures, although having lived in Italy for nearly four years, I can say with certainty that some cultures certainly use gestures more than others! Gestures help us emphasize points, create engagement, and connect with the listener on a nonverbal level. In a business setting, as well as in informal settings, it's critical to incorporate intentional movement to avoid appearing unnatural.

As best practice for a starting position, I recommend loosely clasping your hands at about belly button height. Try interlacing your fingers or tapping the pads of your fingers together, forming a triangle or diamond shape. Either of these positions looks relaxed and comfortable to your audience while also allowing your arms to be ready for movement, so it's easier to raise them for gestures whenever you'd like.

Gestures for Emphasis

When you're speaking, your gestures should underline and emphasize your key points. A two-handed, palms-up gesture works beautifully when you want to show openness or invite the audience to a point of agreement. Alternatively, a single-hand, open-palm gesture is a simple, nonthreatening way to highlight something important.

A word of caution: Avoid pointing with your index finger unless absolutely necessary. Pointing can come across as aggressive or accusatory, which is rarely the effect you want. Similarly, don't keep your hands clasped too low, such as below your belt area, as this draws attention to parts of your body that are not relevant to your message.

What About Microphones and/or Clickers?

If someone offers you a hand-held microphone, ask if there is a Lavalier mic or even a headset instead. Either of these leave your hands free. As soon as you pick up a hand-held microphone, by definition, you lose a limb you can gesture with.

Then, imagine if you are also going to be using a remote clicker to advance through your slides. Now both of your hands will be holding something, which requires you to make a choice about your gestures.

You can't gesture with the hand that holds the microphone because it will move the mic away from your mouth. Keep speaking while you're gesturing away from your face with your mic-holding hand a couple of times and you'll either amuse or annoy your audience as your voice drifts in and out. I've watched uncomfortably as a speaker is up on the stage, unknowingly committing this blunder. I have no idea what they said, as I was too busy listening to the ebb and flow of their sound coming in and out like the tide.

The option here, of course, is to gesture with the hand that is holding the clicker. It's not optimal, with your hand wrapped around the little black plastic device, but it's better than making no gestures at all.

Finally, the *triple threat.* If you're coming to the stage with a tablet or iPad, plus you'll be using a hand-held mic *and* a clicker for your slides, you have a lot to coordinate. It's better here to go ahead and stand behind the podium. Place your iPad on it. Make it easier on yourself. Rehearse many times to get comfortable managing your tech accessories if you're presenting in this situation.

Hands Off: Here's What to Avoid

Some common mistakes presenters make when it comes to hand placement:

- **Hands Behind My Back?** Clasping your hands behind your back can make you seem closed off or detached from your message, so I give this a no-go.
- **Hands in My Pockets?** Digging your hands in your pockets can come across as overly casual or disinterested. It's most often a "man move," but I've seen women do it too. It's usually because you're nervous and don't know what to do with your hands, right? But you do know now.

Remember, you want to be intentional about how your hands are positioned so you remain open and engaged with your audience.

- **Overly Dramatic Gestures?** Overly dramatic gestures, such as fist-pumping, raising your arms overhead, or using aggressive finger-pointing, as I mentioned earlier, can also distract from your message. I recommend you reserve them for a theatrical stage performance, not a professional one. While these actions might feel powerful to you in the moment, they can easily overwhelm or annoy your audience. A good example of a gesture that was once effective but became overused was how Bill Clinton had a habit of gesturing with his thumb pointed upward. I remember watching him do this a lot when he was the US president and I was a young reporter. It may have begun as a substitute for a finger point to the audience—a softer and more thoughtful way to emphasize points—but it quickly became a distracting mannerism that comedians would mimic when they parodied the former US president. You don't want exaggerated gestures to draw attention away from your words.

Practice Makes Progress

To become more confident and comfortable gesturing, practice is essential. I know I've advised this many times before, but I can't stress the power of observation enough. Stand in front of a mirror, or record yourself on your phone, rehearsing your next formal presentation or meeting update delivery. Pay close attention to how you use your hands. Are you gesturing too little or too much? Are your movements enhancing your message or distracting from it? By reviewing yourself, you'll get a sense of how you naturally use your hands and where you can make adjustments.

What If I'm Sitting?

Not all presentations are delivered from the stage. Often, you'll find yourself seated at a table during meetings or panel discussions. In these scenarios, you can still use your hands effectively. Resting your hands on the table with your fingers clasped demonstrates attention and focus. Raising your elbows onto the table and clasping your hands further up can give an even stronger signal that you're actively engaged.

If you want to show a particular level of focus or intensity, you can use a steeple gesture where you bring your index fingers together, leaving your palms open. This is a common and effective technique for showing attentiveness during a discussion.

What you don't want to do is leave your hands in your lap for extended periods. This makes you appear too passive, and in a meeting or on a panel, you don't want to be seen as disengaged. Keeping your hands above the table and in motion (when appropriate) shows that you're part of the conversation, even if you're not speaking at that moment.

Virtual Meetings

Even in a virtual meeting, gestures can add a lot to your presence. If possible, widen your camera frame so that some of your chest is visible, making it easier to bring your hands into the shot. People are more likely to stay focused on what you're saying when they see your hands moving as you speak.

When speaking virtually or in person, avoid covering your mouth with your hand. Not only does it make you harder to hear, but it also sends the message that you might be unsure of what you're saying. Similarly, don't cover your mouth with your hand when you are listening, and don't rest your head on your hand while listening to others—it communicates boredom, and you are making choices to demonstrate better engagement with others at all times.

Activating Your Hands for Better Connection

Your hands are yet another essential tool for enhancing your communication. Whether you're standing on a stage or seated at a conference table, your gestures should always aim to augment your words and build connections with your audience. They can show enthusiasm, invite agreement, or demonstrate authority. But when misused—whether by being too rigid, too dramatic, or too passive—gestures can distract from your message and undermine your effectiveness as a communicator.

Marwa learned to use her hands purposefully, and it made a noticeable difference in how her team perceived her. You, too, can practice controlling your gestures, transforming the way your audience engages with your presentations. Your hands, after all, aren't just there to hang idly at your sides—they're a crucial part of how you convey meaning, build rapport, and create a lasting impact.

Activating your body language awareness to how you stand and where on the stage or in the meeting room, how you walk up onto the stage or into the room, how you sit, and what to do with your hands is all part of *amplifying* your connection with others without saying anything at all.

Is there a difference between purposefully striding on stage wearing a well-fitting dark suit or wearing a tattered pair of jeans and a T-shirt? Of course there is. If you make the effort to power up your body language but you are not also taking more ownership over what attire you wrap your body in, you may be missing opportunities. Because how you show up starts with what you put on. Let's look at the impact of intentional dressing and styling in the next chapter.

Chapter Recap

Click here for a handy demonstration on how best to walk, stand, sit, and gesture.

6 Polish and Power

How Wardrobe and Self-Styling Shape Perception

"When I go out, I'm always dressed up. Not in drag, but always prepared."

—RuPaul

Perception Is Reality Until Proven Otherwise

IT WAS HURRICANE SEASON IN FLORIDA.

I was in Jacksonville, stationed on the beach to cover one of the many storms. Mandatory evacuations were in effect, with seventy-five-mile-per-hour sustained winds roaring around me and a storm surge already churning up to the middle of my thigh.

I was dressed in full-length waders to keep as dry as possible and a set of yellow and black rain gear that I had specifically purchased a couple of weeks prior to this assignment. The surrounding scene was eerie. With the electricity out, the beach felt otherworldly, with only my cameraman and me standing against the elements as waves crashed hard onto the shore.

For about six hours, we'd been doing back-to-back live shots, pushing through relentless wind and water to bring viewers the latest updates. It was exhausting, but I was exhilarated—I was a new reporter, fully committed to delivering a vivid and accurate picture of the storm to those watching from the safety of their homes. Then, suddenly, out of the gray haze, I saw my producer running toward us from the satellite truck, which was parked in a protected area about 100 yards back from the shore. She was struggling through the wind but waved something at me as she got closer—a satellite phone. "The president of CNN wants to talk to you," she said, catching her breath and thrusting the phone toward me. My heart leapt. I was thrilled. I figured he'd noticed my dedication, my hours out in the storm, and that he was calling with words of encouragement or praise.

I pressed the phone to my ear, eager to hear what he had to say. Over the crackling line, his voice finally came through.

What are you wearing out there? You look like a drowned bee.

For a moment, I couldn't believe it. Here I was, in the middle of a hurricane, putting every ounce of my energy into this coverage—and all he could focus on was my appearance. I glanced down at my rain gear, the yellow and black pattern now soaked and clinging to me. It was true; in retrospect, I looked a bit like a bee in that color scheme, but I couldn't shake the frustration. I had been fighting the elements to give my best reporting, and my boss was fixated on my outfit.

What made it even more irritating was that just up the coast, another reporter was also on camera, delivering his own updates. He had ditched traditional rain gear entirely and had wrapped a hotel towel around his head like a turban to keep dry. Somehow, that improvised uniform was seen as acceptable, even endearing, while my outfit—a deliberate, if colorful, choice—was deemed distracting. This wasn't about gender bias—necessarily—it was a lesson in presentation.

If viewers or executives are fixated on what you're wearing, they're not listening to what you're saying.

That moment taught me a vital lesson about the power of clothing to either augment or detract from your message. As a professional, your outfit sends a visual signal before you even open your mouth. Distracting attire can hijack attention from the words you're speaking or the story you're telling. It's not about being flashy or plain; it's about choosing clothes that support the image and message you intend to convey. As much as it frustrated me then, I'm grateful for that call. It helped me understand that:

Like it or not, people take in what they see before they process what they hear.

The Big Debate

I realize there is a big debate about professional attire. Some say that professional attire is essential. Others claim that now, anything goes. That more formal dress is a thing of the past. A few years ago, I watched a late-night TV talk show in which Virgin's famously informally dressed CEO Richard Branson took a pair of scissors and—snip!—cut off the tie that the host was wearing. Of course, he has become the head of a billion-dollar set of companies, so he could do that. I am certain there were times in his younger, less powerful life when he popped on a tie, depending on what person he was going to meet.

The clothing we choose to wear sends a signal to others about where we aspire to go.

Years ago, when I was just starting my career in television news, I had the unenviable job of working overnights. If the morning newscast started at 5:00 a.m., the news crew had to report to the station at midnight. That's the way it was back at WTTG Fox 5 TV in Washington, DC, where I had my first news job.

Reporters arrived wearing their on-air attire, ready for the morning's live broadcasts. But most of the producers, editors, assignment desk people, and writers, like myself, rocked in wearing whatever. They knew the public wouldn't see them on air, so they wore comfortable clothes like jeans, tracksuits, and even pajamas on occasion—I'm not making this up. The executive producer at the time, Susan Truitt, was famous for her Birkenstocks and socks.

But not me. As you already know, from the time I was a girl and had stopped saying *Worsh*ington, I had aspired to be a reporter. Every evening at 11:30 p.m., I woke up and put on something professional, suitable for on-air. A couple of my colleagues jokingly teased me, "All dressed up and nowhere to go."

I admit I looked out of place in that dead-of-night, nearly deserted newsroom, seated at my computer in some snappy outfit surrounded by my super-casual team of co-writers. But one morning, when the field producer for our gregarious weatherman, Tony Perkins, called in sick, my attire gave me an opportunity.

The field producer's job was to be on-site and act as a liaison between the live-shot talent—in this case, Tony—any interview subjects he might meet, and the public who often gathered at the various places of interest where he would be reporting during the two-hour morning show. Although I was a writer at the time who had never filled in as a live-shot field producer before, when the assignment manager looked around the overnight newsroom, guess who looked the part?

I was the only person suitable (get it, suitable? Sorry!) to be allowed out of the overnight newsroom to serve as a substitute for the regular field producer. I happily joined the team and climbed into the news van to drive with Tony and the videographer to the morning's live-shot location.

Let me emphasize this for you. We humans are social animals. We take signals from how other people behave and how people are dressed. A doctor in a white coat. A police officer or firefighter in uniform. Our costumes send others signals.

When RuPaul Charles, the wildly popular drag queen performer and Emmy-award-winning host of the American television show *RuPaul's Drag Race*, was interviewed by the equally famous and award-winning, but much more conservatively dressed host of *The Late Show with Stephen Colbert*, I zeroed in on this telling exchange:

STEPHEN "You said, 'We're all naked. The rest is just drag.'"
RUPAUL "Yes."
STEPHEN "What does that mean? Am I in drag right now?"
RUPAUL "Oh, yes, you are, honey."

STEPHEN "Am I in 'White Man drag'?"
RUPAUL "No, we call this 'Executive Realness.'"

The point RuPaul made is that what we choose to put on our naked bodies before we step out the door sends a message to every single person who sees us. As the saying goes in part, "You can't please all the people all the time." Picture yourself emerging from the gym, visiting the shopping mall, collecting the kids from school, sitting in your college classroom, or arriving for an important presentation. Every outfit you wear gives an impression to others of who you are at the moment. Sometimes, you might not care if the impression is laid back or informal. Other times, it might be essential you exude credibility.

Choosing what you wear with purpose is choosing to show value about yourself and toward others.

Take a moment and consider the clothing you are wearing right now.

Right now, what I am wearing is:

____

____

Right now, the message my clothing is sending is:

____

____

I visited my little brother at his home in Florida right about the time I was working on this chapter. Okay, Brad stands over six feet tall, so he's hardly little. We hadn't seen each other in months, so I told him I was writing a book that contained a chapter encouraging people to strategically consider how to dress more appropriately for different occasions. "That shouldn't matter," he remarked in frustration, echoing what so many others have said.

And one more time, I repeat, I agree.

Attire shouldn't matter. And yet it does.

Imagine you are an employer for a financial institution. Two candidates are competing for one open position. Everything about them is equal.

They have the same qualifications, and they both communicate very well. However, one person showed up for the interview wearing a classic, neutral pair of trousers and a button-down shirt. The other person showed up in a tracksuit. Who are you going to hire?

So, read over the answers you have written above one more time. Try to be impartial. When someone is meeting you for the first time, what do they see?

They cannot see into your heart. They see only what you choose to present. Apparel sends important signals.

How People Perceive You Is Their Reality of You

Remember that training client earlier who said that people need to get to know the real him? Those people are not looking into his soul. They are quickly adding his clothing choices (which consisted of a wrinkly black T-shirt and jeans) into their overall equation of him. That's it.

People pay attention to the clothing you wear. Knowing that, it's essential to think about how you want another person at any given time to perceive you. Remember, the way you perceive others is, for them at least, the reality of who you are.

The feedback they provide you creates an experience for you to react to. **Our lives are made up of our combined feedback loops.** Appearance and clothing are factors that influence those loops.

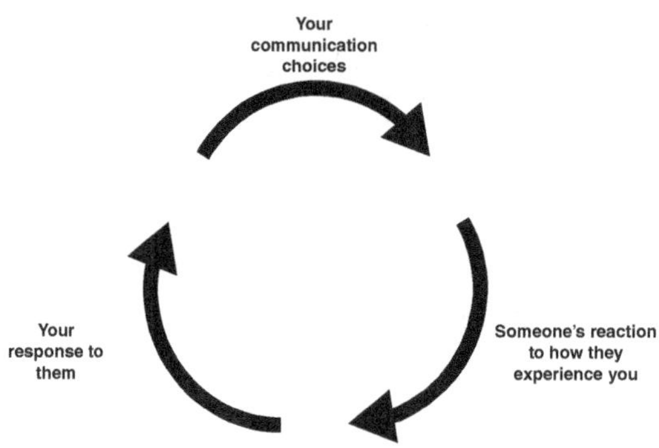

For more on this, I spoke with Maria Macklin from House of Colour, a leading image consultancy based in the United Kingdom. She has helped hundreds of women and men understand how and why to put their best selves forward. "Clothing is your opening paragraph," she explained. "You must take ownership and control over how you are perceived."

You can sabotage yourself if you are not consciously making clothing choices that reflect a confident and poised image of yourself. For instance, when I was speaking about this concept with my friend Neil Gordan, a successful keynote speaking coach who I've worked with, he recalled when he realized his choice to toss on a pair of ripped-up jeans did not help him make the impression he wanted when he walked into an upscale department store.

"I know if I had upped my game just a little, the clerks would have taken me more seriously," he said.

Likewise, let me take you to a classroom full of business students from my college alma mater, Indiana University. It was morning, and they were gathered to listen to me share my story, answer their questions, and then attend a lecture. It wasn't surprising to me that most of them were dressed in typical college fashion: jeans, T-shirts, and emblemed hoodies. But three of them were dressed in business casual attire with slacks and buttoned shirts. They looked sharper than the others, and they stood out. Each of them also demonstrated body language throughout my speech that indicated they were keenly interested (the power of active listening in action) and asked pertinent questions and made thoughtful comments.

There was a fourth young woman in the audience who also seemed extremely engaged through her body language, smiling and occasionally nodding her head. When she asked an insightful question, I could tell she was definitely interested. However, she was also dressed sloppily, which was surprising. She wore a rumpled T-shirt and ripped jeans, similar to my buddy Neil's. Even her hair looked like she'd combed it with an old eggbeater. I imagined she'd overslept as she gave off serious just-rolled-out-of-bed vibes. Her enthusiasm impressed me, but not her image.

Like the interview scenario we imagined together earlier, let's say this bright young woman was competing with any of the other three students I also described. If two candidates were essentially equal in their skills, interview abilities, and even their clothing and grooming choices, with those factors being the only major differences, who would I be less likely to choose to work with or invite to join my organization? It's nothing personal against her, but I think you know the answer.

From department store clerks to interviewers to just about anyone you ever encounter, we make judgments based on what we wear all the time. Assuming you want to put your best version of yourself forward—to *amplify* the person you are within—how do you take more control of your wardrobe choices? First: prepare in advance. Take some time to think about your audience.

Research Your Target's Clothing Culture

Do your research. What is the corporate clothing culture where you will be visiting? Look at the company's website. What is their executive team wearing in their About Us photos? I suggest, if you're meeting for an interview or any sort of introductory face-to-face, wearing something at the same level or even one step up will create the positive visual perception you are aiming for. When you appear poised through proper clothing choices, it instills confidence in you for others.

Obviously, you will dress differently if you are going to meet with the head of a bank rather than the head of the contemporary art museum. It's safe to say you will have more clothing freedom of expression when you are taking part in the art world than if you are seeking a career or advancement in the financial world. Aim to keep your attire a sharp and intentional version of either.

Also, pay attention to the gravity of the particular communication event you will be attending. Think of your audience first! If the event is lighthearted, like a team picnic or an informal networking event, your appearance and attire may gently reflect that. If the event is serious, like a first interview or an industry-wide economic conference or a company gala awards dinner event, your appearance should reflect that.

As my House of Colour expert underlined, "You can't go wrong with classic."

Clothing is one of the most immediate ways we communicate to the world who we are. From suits to scarves, what we wear can reflect our professionalism, values, and respect for those around us. When dressing for work, or anywhere really, I encourage you to balance your choices to express your individuality while also aligning with the context of the industry, country, or organizational culture where you find yourself.

Gina of Arabia

The first time I traveled to Saudi Arabia was in 2021. Riyad Bank invited me to give a workshop on team leadership and gamification at their headquarters. Although I was aware that the country's announced Vision 2030 plan included loosening restrictions for women, like allowing them to drive and to work alongside their male counterparts in the same office spaces, I wasn't sure what the acceptance level was for Western women over what to wear and whether to cover their hair.

I was fortunate to have had experience working in the Middle East when I lived in Egypt in 2006. Back then, most Egyptian women chose to cover their arms and legs with an *abaya* and their hair with a *hijab*, but there were those who chose not to. In fact, I remember listening with interest to a discussion in my office between two Egyptian women, both practicing Muslims, over the advantages and disadvantages of covering. The older woman was adamantly against the practice, and the other, younger woman, defended it as part of their culture. I refrained from entering the conversation as it was not my culture, but when I walked through the public streets of Cairo, I always wore long-sleeved shirts along with skirts or trousers that reached my ankles. I rarely covered my hair.

Now, several years later, and about to enter a part of the region previously known for its much more stringent rules on the matter, I chose to err on the side of caution. I borrowed an abaya and hijab from a Sudanese friend and packed it in my suitcase. Then, before the flight touched down in Riyadh, I ducked into the airplane's lavatory and layered myself with the gown and the scarf.

There were only a couple of other Western women getting off the plane with me and lining up for passport control at the King Khalid International Airport. Both of them were wearing long-sleeved pantsuits. Neither had their hair covered. The national women who were operating the customs counters at the airport, however, were completely enshrouded. I kept my scarf on. Later, when I checked into the registration desk at the Hilton hotel, I asked the man at the desk if it was required or encouraged.

"Modest dress is encouraged," he explained in perfect English. "But it doesn't need to be the abaya. And for Western women and your hair, no covering of any kind is required or expected."

But I'm still glad I made my initial choice to do so on both counts. Wherever I am traveling, I am a guest of that country and that country's culture. It may be evolving, but I am not there to push it along faster or further through my clothing choices. I am not there to make disruptive fashion waves or even ripples. I am there to try to connect with others on a peer-to-peer, respectful, and professional level.

What we wear sends a message: How we respect others and how we can expect others to respect us.

Okay, let's dig in. First up: remember, accountability—not conformity—is key. You can still express yourself in a way that respects other cultures, colleagues, clients, customers, and the public.

Getting Back to Basics

For men and women, suits, shirts, trousers, and dresses are often seen as the go-to symbols of professionalism, with subtle nuances in style and fit conveying different messages. A dark, solid-colored suit, for example, suggests a level of polish and readiness—often expected in more traditional fields like finance, law, or government. However, a well-fitted pair of pants paired with a neat shirt or blouse can project similar professionalism in more casual industries. The key lies in selecting pieces that fit well and are in good condition. Any reasonably priced outfit can look elevated if it fits you well and is worn with confidence.

A Word About Accessories

Personal items like socks, tights, or stockings can either blend in or offer a touch of personality. A pair of patterned socks or colored tights can introduce a pop of individuality, particularly in creative industries or workplaces where originality is valued. However, in more formal settings, classic colors might be more appropriate to convey a steady, reliable image. The goal isn't to suppress your personality but to be mindful of when and how it is shown.

I don't want you to overthink each of these things, but be aware that your jewelry, too, offers a way to add flair while remaining professional. Small earrings or a delicate necklace can add elegance without overpowering the outfit. If you choose large, dangly earrings, be aware you are sending a louder signal and adjust accordingly.

I recently attended a lunchtime gathering that featured Steve Pagliuca, the co-owner of the Boston Celtics. The team had clinched a record-setting eighteenth National Basketball Association (NBA) championship in the United States. And here was Steve, proudly wearing the largest, most attention-grabbing ring I had ever seen. It was nearly three inches in diameter, full of sparkle and bling. It commemorated the team's prestigious NBA title, and there was no way the moderator of the fireside chat with Steve would be able to ask about anything else before that ring. None of us in the audience could focus on anything else.

Steve graciously explained what a thrill it was to be wearing such a showstopper and that the ring even opened up like a locket to reveal a small stadium with the dates of each of the previous Celtics league championships. You may not possess something quite as dramatic, but be aware that flashy adornments will be a distraction. It's up to you to wear them with pride, like Steve, or choose to leave them at home.

Likewise, you can choose a tasteful or more flamboyant necktie, or perhaps not wear one at all. Your watch may also send a signal. Other items, such as neck scarves, hats, and bow ties, are also expressive accessories that, if styled thoughtfully, can bring personality to an outfit without detracting from what is hopefully your top-tier messages: credibility, connection, and competence. Tattoos and body piercings are increasingly accepted, particularly in younger, creative workspaces, though it's wise to gauge if covering them up initially might be more respectful if you are interacting with more conservative clients or leaders.

Well-Designed Clothing Does Not Need to Be Designer

Many affordable brands offer sleek, professional attire and classic pieces that you can mix and match for a variety of looks. As I've already said, knowing your audience and dressing accordingly isn't about suppressing your creativity. Rather, it's about refining it in a way that both expresses your individuality and respects the environment you're in.

Dressing professionally does not mean spending beyond your means. In fact, the notion that only designer clothes can create a polished appearance isn't true. I'm here to encourage you to choose clothing that not only fits well, suits your style, and is appropriate for the setting, but is also appropriate for your income level. Whether you're shopping at a high-end retailer, a department store, or a thrift shop, the key lies in selecting pieces thoughtfully and focusing on versatility rather than brand names.

For instance, a plain, well-fitted blazer or a pair of clean trousers that you can press when you get home can be found at almost any price point. Buying fewer high-quality basics rather than a large wardrobe filled with fast fashion is more economical and sustainable. Likewise, if you prefer dresses or skirts, a mix of neutrals like black, navy, taupe, and gray can create multiple outfits, which will save you both money and time.

Tailoring is another affordable strategy that often gets overlooked. Even an inexpensive pair of trousers or a dress can look higher-end with a bit of alteration. For a relatively small investment, a seamstress or tailor can adjust hems, sleeves, and fits to flatter your body, making budget-friendly items look polished and custom-fitted. This attention to fit can make a huge difference in how you're perceived. It can signal that you have an eye for detail and commitment to presenting your best self, regardless of where the clothes originally came from.

When I was a network correspondent for CNN, I received a small annual stipend for clothing, and a stylist helped me select classics that would last. Over the years, when I was living in Denver and no longer had the luxury of that allowance, I found great success shopping at a nearby consignment store that was frequented by the wives of the Denver Broncos football players. These ladies dropped off designer labels I would never have been able to afford at full price. I picked them up, had them altered to give me a better fit, and voila, I felt like a million dollars for a fraction of the original price.

Thrifting and second-hand stores can be fantastic resources, particularly if you're seeking unique pieces like vintage blazers, classic blouses, or unique accessories that can add character to your outfits without breaking the bank. As with my consignment shop in Denver, many vintage and resale shops can be gold mines for finding well-made, timeless pieces that suit both casual and formal work settings.

Personal Care Is Professional Flair

When it comes to presenting our most professional selves, hair and makeup are another area where we can show personal style in a polished way that reflects both our personality and respect for those around us. I'm not here to say that men must keep their hair short or that anyone needs to hide their natural textures. Quite the opposite—I encourage you to embrace your look.

Whether you wear it smooth, curly, in waves, cropped, or as an afro, the key is keeping your hair well maintained, to say, "I respect myself, and I respect you."

Your hair can be your canvas to express who you are. For men and women alike, clean, groomed hair makes a difference. A bit of maintenance, whether that's a trim, a fresh wash, or simply ensuring your look feels intentional, can help you look as professional as you feel.

For those of you who, like me, prefer longer styles, keeping the ends healthy or neatly styled can do wonders. Shorter cuts, when kept sharp and fresh, can convey a sense of energy and readiness. Natural curls, coils, and textures are beautiful as they are, requiring only a bit of attention to keep them at their best. No matter your style, it's about creating an intentional look to *amplify* the wonderful you inside.

Makeup can also be a tool to highlight your individuality. You don't need a full-face glam look unless that's your preference, and it won't distract your audience. A subtle touch can go a long way: a bit of concealer, a sweep of mascara, or a quick pop of color on the lips can brighten up the face and give you a fresh, awake look with little fuss. If you like bolder or fuller coverage for your makeup, play with colors and shapes that make you feel like the most confident version of yourself, always ensuring the look is appropriate for your setting. Think of it as framing and highlighting your best features rather than trying to cover anything up.

Connecting Cleanliness and Confidence

And let's not forget the small but essential details, like clean nails, brushed teeth, and fresh deodorant. Regardless of your style, these small steps show you've put care into how you present yourself. Well-groomed nails—whether bare, polished with a nude shade, or boldly colored—are simple but effective. Similarly, a little attention to personal freshness, like deodorant or a touch of fragrance, conveys a quiet message that you're mindful of others. These details might seem minor, but they often leave a lasting impression.

Your goal here is not to look or even smell like everyone else, it's showing a level of care that reflects positively on you and lets others know you respect the shared space you find yourself in.

Make a List and Check It Twice

Over the years, many of my clients who are unsure about how to begin building or updating their wardrobe and grooming have asked me to help them. I have prepared lookbooks for people from Seattle to Singapore.

So, let's work through a short checklist to help you make decisions more quickly, take control over what you choose to put or not put on your body, and what each choice may transmit to others about you. (Remember, as with every recommendation in this book, your awareness and understanding of the situation, your audience, and yourself will help inform your intentional decision-making.)

Appearance Checklist

- ✓ What's the occasion?
- ✓ Where are you going?
- ✓ What country? What state? What city?
- ✓ Will you sit in a rural setting? Urban?
- ✓ Is it a daytime event? A nighttime awards dinner?
- ✓ An internal sales meeting? An offsite team-building weekend?
- ✓ Your first interview with a company?
- ✓ Are you going to be outside? Might there be a wind? If so, what can you do to compensate? (I once reported live for CNN from a very windy scene during tornado season in Kansas with gaffer tape covering the back of my head to prevent my hair from flying forward like a boat's sail. If you're outside for an interview or some event in the wind, you may want to consider another option. I can assure you it was painful to pull that tape off!) Your clothing choices should reflect the culture of the environment in which you appear.
- ✓ Who are the people you will be meeting?

We will thoroughly explore my notion of relationship architecture and my AIM preparation strategy in Part III, but for now, ask yourself:

- ✓ How well do you know this person or people?
- ✓ Are they senior leaders? Are they junior?

✓ What clothing choices will accentuate or *amplify* the version of you that is likely to best connect with them?

Let's Talk More About Clothing Choices

Plan ahead. When in doubt, choose your favorite, well-fitting classic outfit rather than trying something new and unproven for the first time. Unless you're sure of the positive impact you will create, leave loud patterns, T-shirts with logos, oversized bows, shark-skin suits, and any unflattering or outdated pieces at home unless you are prepared to explain why this supports your brand and will best connect you to the people at the event.

Monochrome is usually perceived more positively than busy patterns. Neutral colors are more classic. Bright colors will draw more attention, which you may or may not want.

Buttoned shirts and ties without a jacket are usually fine. Add the jacket and you're now that much more serious. A jacket, shirt, and no tie is also okay, but just understand the image you are projecting, the culture you are representing, and the audience you are speaking to.

- **Is your attire culture-conscious?**
  Cultural wardrobe considerations are absolutely essential. If your country's culture requires or encourages particular garments, then act accordingly.

  Similarly, if you hail from a place where traditional dress is an alternative for business—like many countries across Africa, for example—wearing traditional dress as an option may be perfectly suitable, especially if you are from the region in which the event is taking place.

  If you are from Ghana and living in Germany and plan to interview for a position within a conservative bank in Berlin, you might want to consider dressing more classically Western because it reflects that company's corporate culture.

  Make an informed decision and go with it.
- **Will you be on camera?**
  When interviewed on camera, avoid herringbone and other small patterns as they may cause camera focus lenses to strobe. Consider

the background colors if you are on set, and choose colors that contrast or complement. What will the host or interviewer be wearing? (I could write a book about working with the media. Maybe next time.)

- **With accessories, less is usually more.**
  Are your shoes polished and not scuffed? Ladies, make sure there are no broken nails protruding out of your high heels. Are your earrings overpowering your face? Generally speaking, leave the chandeliers and giant hoops for the disco, not the office.
- **Are you body conscious?**
  Make sure your nails, eyebrows, ears, and nose hairs are all trimmed, you have showered, and you're wearing deodorant or antiperspirant. Being body-conscious is not the same thing as being body-self-conscious. I don't want you to feel insecure, but I want you to take this stuff more seriously than perhaps you have up until now because you *can* take more control of the version of you that you intentionally choose to bring to any occasion.

Classic = Confidence.
How you dress becomes part of your brand.

As with body language, the choices you make about your wardrobe and the routine you have for grooming and personal hygiene all speak volumes as soon as you walk in the door, before you utter a single word. There's a certain amount of consideration and preparation that should accompany every choice you make.

As you turn the page to Part III, "Be It!," you'll begin connecting your awareness with strategic preparation and putting it all into action.

You've honed your awareness, sharpened your presence, and aligned your outward signals to showcase your best self. Now, it's time to dig into the real strategy: learning to intentionally shape your behavior to build stronger connections and open those doors.

Think of this upcoming section as your toolkit for amplified influence: practical techniques that can help you spark trust, engage others, and make a lasting impact in any room you walk into.

PART 3 Be It!

7 Taking AIM

The (Surprisingly) Overlooked Power Move of Communication

"The need for change bulldozed a road down the center of my mind."

—Maya Angelou

You Can Take More Control

IT'S NOW TIME TO TURN SOMETHING YOU'RE READING INTO SOMETHING YOU'RE DOING.

Let's put all the pieces together and apply them. I'd love for you to feel like saying: "Okay, Gina, you've convinced me that I can purposefully learn to think, speak, and appear in a more amplified way. I can develop myself *not* to live my life as an actor on stage wearing a mask, but instead to purposely become the version of myself that will better connect with my fellow humans. I am identifying each element of my human-ness so that one by one, I can take more control of them. I am learning how to *amplify* the power within me."

I can human-up.

I hope that's what you're thinking right now as you proceed into the "Be It!" section. I hope so because I am already celebrating you as you are now, and the amped-up person you are becoming.

Being it is the evolution that transpires after we turn the thoughts, techniques, and approaches into action.

These actions are experienced by ourselves and others when:

- We change our *thoughts* about ourselves to be more positive.
- We select more impactful *words* by reducing jargon, simplifying, powering up, or speaking more from the heart.
- We play our *voice* like the instrument it was intended to be.
- We deliver more positive and intentional *body language* by taking control of our expressions, movements, and gestures.
- We *wear* what reinforces our message—polished, purposeful, and aligned with how we want to be perceived.

Being authentic doesn't mean we say anything we want to anyone at any time we want. Ancient Roman leader and Stoic philosopher Marcus Aurelius understood this thousands of years ago when he wrote that people don't need to have an opinion about everything. Or, as modern philosopher and author Ryan Holiday said during a recent lecture I attended in Dublin:

"You don't have to say 'yuck' to everyone's 'yum.'"[1]

Sometimes, we hold our tongues, and that's okay.

We are committed to being in the driver's seat of our career and our life. We are not aimlessly floating in a boat on a rapidly rushing river. We are crafting our own oars, paddles, and even a motor. We know that:

We are communicating all the time.

I keep saying this because I want to remind you that you are never off. We all sometimes think *I'm not in the mood; I'm going to switch off.* Remember, if someone is with you in a real or virtual room, even if you're not saying anything, you're still communicating. Unless you're alone in that room watching Netflix or taking a well-deserved nap, you are still most definitely on.

It doesn't matter whether you are addressing your organization's board, talking to someone at the lunch table, on a bus, in an Uber, ordering pizza, disciplining your child, or house-training your dog. Every time you interact with another being, you have the opportunity to move your relationship and reputation with them either forward or backward.

Our communications are never neutral.

So, given how important ongoing communication is, I encourage you to spend more time learning to be intentional about all this. By learning about the range of communication choices that are in your power to select, you can better consider them and implement them at the right time for each situation.

Let's re-examine the three areas in which a person is taking note of their perceptions of you during any communications event. A three-legged stool is the image I use for my clients. Each leg is equally important.

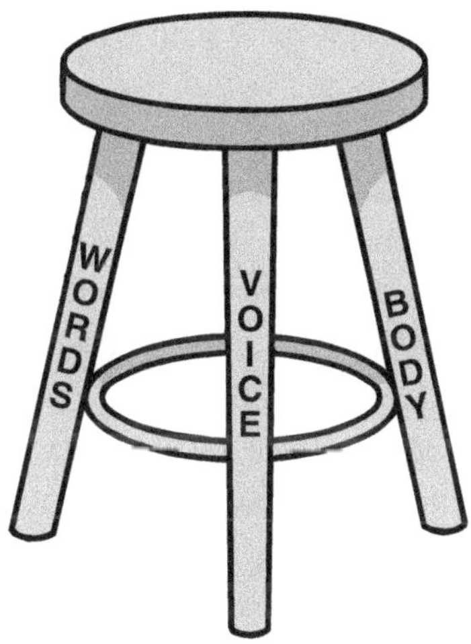

Imagine the first leg is our **words**.

The second leg is our **voice**.

And the third leg is our **body language**.

A lot of business professionals will focus primarily on content. But they don't think enough about choosing the connecting words or weaving in their voice and body to the emotions behind the words.

The Mehrabian Myth
"You've heard it before: 93% of communication is nonverbal. That's oversimplified. It's the harmony of your nonverbals plus your words which will set you apart."

Some people will claim that the three legs don't work in balance and that we should be dedicating most of our development time toward our vocal tonality and our body language. They'll often reference what I call the Mehrabian Myth (Albert Mehrabian[2] is a prominent psychologist best known for his research on nonverbal communication). You've probably heard this before: 55% of communication is body language, 38% is tone of voice, and only 7% is the actual words. It's repeated so often, it sounds like a hard fact. But it's not. It's a major oversimplification of Albert Mehrabian's research—and it was never meant to apply to every kind of communication.

Let's bust this myth once and for all. Mehrabian's 1967 study centered on the way people can change *single words* with tone and facial expressions, not longer forms of communication. He was researching how people respond when a message's tone and body language conflict with the words being spoken. For example, in one of his studies, he had the speaker deliver the single word *dear* with a flat tone and furrowed brow. Of course, the listener correctly inferred that the intent of the word was more negative due to the combination of how it was packaged. But this doesn't mean that body language and tone always combine to account for 93% of every communication exchange.

My friend, researcher and author Nick Morgan,[3] blows steam from his ears when he hears this misrepresentation. As he points out, imagine watching a movie in a language you don't speak—with no subtitles—and trying to get 93% of the meaning through tone and gestures alone. It doesn't work. Sure, you'd pick up on a few emotions, but you'd miss all the nuance, context, and actual content. Words *do* matter, especially when the topic is complex or intellectual.

Therefore, imagine again our three-legged stool. Communication is a balance of all three elements: words, body language, and tone. When they work together, they *amplify* you and your message. They each help you *Be It!* Mehrabian never intended for his percentages to be applied so broadly. So, next time you hear someone quote Mehrabian out of context, feel free to set the record straight!

We can all benefit from actively considering how our words, our voice, and our bodies are in synchronicity all the time.

When you put all three legs of the stool into synergistic action, when you *be* it, you will *be*come the person who radiates connection. When you activate your observer mentality while around other people—be it in group meetings or grocery shopping—tasks that may have held little to no learning or growth opportunities before will begin to take on new meaning because you will be more engaged.

You will become less *self-conscious* because you are more *others-conscious*. You will begin to take action to cultivate your curiosity for others every day. Small talk will no longer be purposeless, but more like a game of hide-and-seek where you are searching for a common interest or a shared experience—an opportunity to build understanding and rapport with another person.

You are not developing soft skills. These are the critical skills required to become more human and bring more humanity into the workplace and into your everyday life. As I've mentioned before, with the rise of artificial intelligence and machine learning, these bits of technology will never replace your personal "connectability" unless you refuse to activate who you are. (I know "connectability" is not actually a word, but it should be!)

How far you are into this book tells me you're a leader. Leaders aren't just about being a boss or a manager; leaders inspire others to take action and identify the genius inside. As author and researcher Liz Wiseman writes in her best-selling book *Multipliers*:[4]

"Multipliers invoke each person's unique intelligence and create an atmosphere of genius—innovation, productive effort, and collective intelligence."

—Liz Wiseman

Ready Your AIM

I am enthusiastic to introduce you to the AIM methodology:

Audience
Intent
Message

A simple yet powerful tool that will serve as the foundation of your three-legged stool for confident, effective communication.

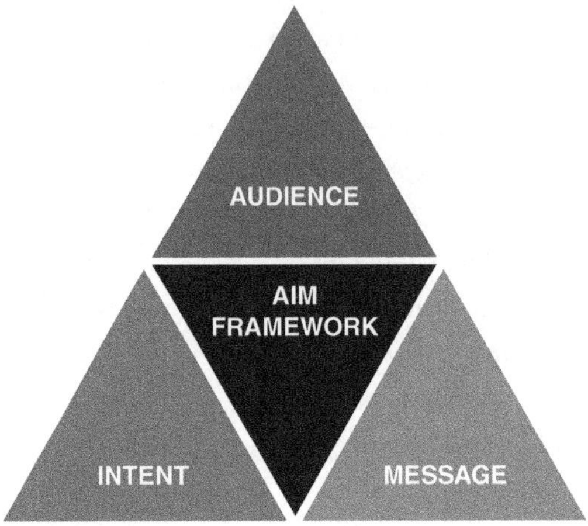

Developed through years of experience and research, I first came across this when I was co-training with a fellow former TV news journalist, Aileen Pincus,[5] in Washington, DC. I later read more about it through the teaching of J. D. Schramm[6] during his time with the Stanford Graduate School of Business. AIM is a flexible framework that applies to every type of communication event, from high-stakes presentations to informal daily interactions.

While the process of preparing for these interactions may vary depending on the scenario, the order of AIM always remains the same. We start by understanding our *audience*, move to clarify our *intent*, and then, finally, shape our *message*.

Audience: Understanding Who They Are and What They Need

Why begin with the audience? Because understanding those we are communicating with is the surest way to build trust and make a lasting impact. Before focusing on what we want to convey, we need to understand who is receiving it and why. When we invest time in understanding our audience, we can communicate in a way that respects their needs, preferences, and perspectives. This initial focus on others helps reduce self-consciousness and increases our connection with those we engage with. In essence, the more others-conscious we become, the more powerfully we can "be it."

Most people instinctively focus first on crafting what they want to say, effectively prioritizing their own perspectives and insights over those of their listeners. But before we formulate any message, it's essential to pause and consider: *Who is my audience? What are their needs, interests, and motivations?*

The audience is always the starting point because, without understanding who you are going to be talking to, even the most carefully crafted messages can miss the mark.

Imagine the Pictures in the Other Person's Head

Audience analysis goes beyond basic demographics such as age, gender, or role. Instead, it encourages a deeper examination of what educator and Pulitzer Prize winner Stuart Diamond calls in his best-selling book *Getting More*,[7] "the pictures in their heads"—those unique beliefs, motivations, and emotional responses that shape what people are thinking in the time they're listening to you. These things will, of course, impact how they receive your message.

"The single biggest problem in communication is the illusion that it has taken place."

—George Bernard Shaw

Each person is different. A new client might be full of skepticism or excitement, while an established colleague could carry a wealth of background knowledge on your topic but may lack enthusiasm for further input. Adjusting for these factors ensures that you *meet your listeners where they are, not where you think they should be.*

People are even different at various times of the day or days of the week. Imagine, for instance, if you're planning to talk to a colleague or supervisor (or anyone for that matter) before breakfast on the first day of the week, or after lunch on the last day of the week. Are they hungry? Tired? Ready to go home?

I know I feel fresh in the early morning before the business of the day saps my energy. As my teenage daughter knows, if you want to convince me of something, it's better to find me in the morning than in the evening. When she sat me down with a PowerPoint presentation about why I should buy her a puppy, she did it first thing in the morning *after* she brought me a cup of coffee. Smart girl. At the time of this writing, our mini-schnauzer Pepper has been part of our family for five years already.

If something is impacting the mindset of your target audience, consider their points of view before you draft any kind of message, whether it's on paper, on your laptop, or in your head.

The Importance of Audience Mapping

In my coaching sessions, I often work with clients who are preparing for high-profile presentations or important policy discussions. I encourage them to write down their agenda as they originally envisioned it, then, on a separate page, rewrite that agenda as they believe their audience would prioritize it. This process of audience mapping often reveals significant discrepancies between the two versions, emphasizing the importance of revising the order in which you will work through content based on the audience's needs. Throw out your agenda and proceed with the one you created based on your best understanding of their point of view.

Take Mark, one of my executive clients. He was preparing to present a major company reorganization. After thinking about what his team would be most worried about—things like job security and how their day-to-day work would change—he decided to start his talk by addressing those concerns right away. By leading with clear answers and reassurance, he made sure his audience could actually hear the rest of his message.

Because if people are fixated on something else, they won't really be listening to you.

Relationship Architecture: Climbing the Eiffel Tower of Communications

A crucial element when you're analyzing how you may want to approach an audience is to first consider what I describe as your **relationship architecture**. Just as an architect designs a building based on the environment, materials, and purpose, we must build our communication approach based on our relationship with our audience. When we consider how well we know our listeners, what kind of rapport exists, and what style they respond to, we lay a strong foundation that makes our communication more effective and resonant.

Imagine the Eiffel Tower.

When you are planning to interact with someone new or in a formal setting, picture yourself at the base of the tower. You don't know them well enough to crack the first joke that comes into your head or come to the meeting wearing your worn-out sneakers. Instead, you should proceed with a more careful and formal approach. It's always better to show professionalism and respect.

For example, when I first worked with a new freelance videographer who was going to be recording one of my presentations, I noticed his laptop was covered in stickers. Some were funny, some were irreverent, and a couple were downright inappropriate. Luckily, I noticed this while we were setting up before the clients arrived. We covered the laptop so no one saw it. This is a prime example of how being better safe than sorry can work for you when you're actively taking ownership of how you care for your audience—especially in critical first-time communications.

Another time, I was meeting with a new client. He was a young man who I was to help prepare for an upcoming pitch to potential high-level investors. I could see he was wearing two earrings during our virtual session. While I appreciated his expression of individuality, I suggested he consider whether he'd wear the same look for his first meeting with those financial prospects, particularly as their culture might favor conservative appearances. He agreed to leave the earrings behind for the initial meetings. But he chose to wear them around their third meeting once he established rapport. This was a considered choice, aligned with how he progressed up our figurative Eiffel Tower—as he built credibility and trust.

When you are with people who know you extremely well, and you have loads of trust, maybe your dearest family or friends, or even colleagues you have gone through the trenches with, you are standing together at the top of that tower. These are established relationships, so it's very safe to adopt a more casual tone, wear your sneakers, and express ideas with more familiarity. At this lofty height you can probably even break out your corny, but never rude, humor.

When someone knows you well, they are more likely to respond positively to an informal approach. Imagine you're briefing a trusted, long-time colleague about a new project. Here, you can dispense with formalities, focusing instead on honest dialogue and mutual brainstorming. But if you're onboarding a junior or new team member, you should strike a bit more formal approach. You should still be pleasant, of course, but not overly familiar.

Over time, as you understand each other's styles and motivations, you'll find yourself engaging in more meaningful exchanges—ones that would be impossible in a purely formal setting.

Just like with the Eiffel Tower, as your rapport strengthens, it's like you're walking up another flight of steps. Keep aiming to move up.

The higher the vantage point, the more mutual understanding and the more flexibility you will achieve in your communication style.

Paying attention to your relationship architecture gives you the flexibility to adapt, which can deepen your connections by meeting people at their comfort level.

When you're considering the A in AIM—taking time to try to understand your audience—it also means getting tuned in to their emotional landscape. People's moods, stresses, and mental states affect their openness to your message.

Hopes, Dreams, and Fears

When I was training to be a television anchor, I was flown to a training school in Texas. There, I had to cold read (reading with no advance rehearsal) a variety of news scripts from the teleprompter.

I remember that one script in particular was, to me, a rather bland stock-market report. I read the copy in a similar bland tone. My coach stopped me mid-sentence and reminded me that even seemingly flat statistics are likely to affect real people somewhere. "Every story has a hope, a dream, or a fear," he told me.

This insight shifted my approach entirely. I began reading with an awareness that my tone could either reassure viewers or add to their worries. I didn't overly evoke here, but I did pay more attention. That's how we need to consider our audiences, too. What are their hopes, dreams, or fears? We don't want to prey on any fears, of course. This book is about encouraging you to be a communicator with positive impact—someone who seeks to unite and reassure, not to instill fear, anger, or division.

Balancing Credibility and Warmth

Developing an audience-first mindset does more than clarify your message; it builds trust and establishes your credibility. As human-centric leaders, we should aim for a balance between credibility and warmth.

People who feel considered and respected by your approach are more likely to listen, engage, and respond positively. A speaker who demonstrates that they've thought about their listeners' perspectives fosters a connection that is invaluable in leadership.

So, before you even think about your message, pause and ask yourself:

- *Who is my audience?*
- *How well do I know them?*
- *What might they be feeling right now?*

When you make your audience the focal point, your communication becomes more relevant, empathetic, and impactful.

In the next sections, we'll continue this journey by examining the I in AIM—*intent*, exploring why it's essential to define your goal and purpose for each communication. Then we'll discuss the *message*, where we bring our audience and intent together to create clear, memorable, and compelling messages.

But always remember: AIM starts with the audience. Because until we fully understand *who* we're speaking to, we can never be certain *how* we should be speaking.

Intent: Moving Beyond Information

We've covered the audience, now it's time to move on to intent. Intent is often mistaken for information, but let's be clear that intent isn't merely delivering data or facts. Instead, intent is something more dynamic and purposeful.

Intent is about sparking an action, a mindset shift, or even a question that encourages your audience to take a step beyond where they started with you. When your intent, goal, or outcome is clear and finely tuned, it becomes the driving force that makes your communication memorable and impactful.

This is about moving someone to do something as a result of hearing what you say.

It could be as simple as encouraging your audience to ask for more details, or as direct as prompting them to agree on a major decision or policy. Defining your *intent* means envisioning the *action* you want to see happen immediately after you've delivered your message, and it involves more precision than most people realize.

Focus on the Immediate, Achievable Action

A strong intent should not be cluttered with too many competing objectives. Imagine you're wrapping up a talk. If your intent involves a laundry list of actions or changes, your audience may end up feeling overwhelmed or unsure of where to start.

Intent is powerful when it's focused. The clearer and more specific the intent, the more likely it is to lead to action.

Let me give you an example: I've seen clients sometimes attempt to cram multiple objectives into one meeting. They end up trying to make their audience understand a new policy, adopt a fresh set of standards, and agree on a second meeting—all in one go. But when you load up an audience with too many points, the actual purpose gets lost, and your audience will likely go back to their desks and fall back into old habits. Instead, by defining a single, achievable outcome, you are far more likely to leave a lasting impression.

Sometimes, the intent can be as simple as securing an agreement for a follow-up conversation or a second meeting. Don't underestimate the power of breaking large objectives down into smaller, bite-sized steps. A single, achievable outcome clarifies your purpose and makes it easier for your audience to say yes to that next step.

Aligning Intent for Collective Clarity: My Story from Sweden

In 2019, I spent a great deal of time traveling back and forth to Stockholm, where I was working with a senior leadership team for a large company headquartered there. The stakes were high as they were preparing for a major organizational change in response to an activist shareholder's pressure. The new policies were going to impact all employees, and each of the leaders had their own ideas about how to approach this rollout. When I walked into that meeting, the table was covered with papers, notes, and presentations—a real flurry of information.

Each leader told me they had a clear vision for their part, but as we started the discussion, it also became clear that each of the five senior team members had subtly different ideas of what they wanted employees to do once this information was presented. One wanted employees to understand the reasoning behind the change, another wanted them to focus on the timeline, while another still wanted everyone to grasp the financial implications. They were each aiming to inform, but without one cohesive intent, their message would likely become overwhelming for the employees receiving it.

I stepped in and said, "Let's take a moment. Before we refine any further, let's go around the room, and I want each of you to articulate exactly what you want employees to *do* as a result of this meeting."

We went around, and each leader explained their intended outcome—some focused on knowledge, others on understanding, and others on unity. This simple act of verbalizing the intended outcome brought clarity to the team. They saw that although their intents overlapped, they each had different priorities.

That moment of alignment made all the difference. They soon agreed on a single intent that they all could reinforce. Their unified intent was to build confidence in the company's strategy and ensure that *all* employees felt valued in the process. By refining their intent to a single, collective purpose, they could all support each other's roles, creating a much more streamlined, impactful approach.

Had we not taken that time to clarify, they would have likely walked out with a muddled message. Instead, they emerged with a cohesive, actionable goal.

Defining Intent Clearly—and Out Loud

This part is essential. It's not enough to just *think* about your intent. Write it down, and if you're working in a team, say it out loud. Each person should have a shared understanding, especially when multiple people are delivering a message. It's amazing how often misalignment on intent surfaces only when we finally vocalize our goals.

The exercise I used in Sweden wasn't only about getting the team to agree on their messaging. It was a way to build buy-in on the action they hoped to inspire. When everyone actually voiced their goals, it forced them to clarify and make a choice: What's the one thing they wanted employees to do immediately after their presentation?

Consider the Timeline of Interactions

Setting intent also means thinking about where this particular message sits on the timeline of your relationship with your audience. Is this a first encounter, where you might want to build trust before asking for too much? Or have you already established a rapport, and now it's time to propose a next-level action?

In Sweden, the leadership team knew that this wasn't the first time they were bringing a new policy to employees. They were experienced, and they knew their audience might be weary of another presentation on change. So, they needed to recognize where this message would fit within the company's ongoing dialogue with employees. Acknowledging their employees and expressing their understanding helped them shape an intent that felt realistic and achievable within that context.

Intent as a "North Star" for Communication

Intent acts as your North Star in communication. When you set an intent, you gain the ability to prioritize content and make meaningful decisions on what to include and what to leave out. This guiding purpose prevents you from wandering off topic or overwhelming your audience with unrelated information. Every part of your message should contribute to the intended outcome, and anything that doesn't serve that purpose should be left out.

How do you show up?
How do you get a little better every day?

With a clear intent in place, you can start crafting a message that's both purposeful and powerful. Remember, the intent isn't the message itself; it's what you want your message to achieve. Each word, example, and explanation you use should bring the audience closer to that goal. So, now let's explore how to best craft those words to achieve that.

Message: Meaningful, Memorable, and Actionable

Once you've defined your intent with laser precision, it's time to turn that clarity into a compelling, actionable message. A message is your call to action or an inspirational takeaway that your audience can easily grasp, repeat, and act upon. It's not the entire content of your talk or presentation. Rather, it's the anchor point, the essence you want them to carry forward long after your time on stage or in a meeting ends.

A well-crafted message is like a musical chorus—something that resonates, lingers, and has the power to move people to take real steps based on the words you deliver.

For many of my clients, narrowing their message to a single, cohesive statement can be surprisingly challenging. They may think they have a message, only to find that it's more of a theme or a broad goal rather than a clear, actionable point. But clarity and precision are key here. Without these, you risk leaving your audience unsure about what you want them to actually *do* as a result of your words.

The Value of Precision: A Lesson with a CTO

A client I've partnered with for many years is the chief technology officer of one of the largest construction companies in the world. We were preparing for an interview with a prominent business reporter, and I asked him, "Have you crafted a strong, clear message for this interview?" He assured me he had. Yet when the interview began, I listened closely as my reporter friend asked questions, and my client responded, and I never heard him actually land a message.

The interview went smoothly. My client was articulate, and he shared many insights. But afterward, when I asked, "At what point did you actually land your message?" he admitted, "Well, I didn't have a specific message, but I had a theme." That's a common pitfall. A theme is not a message. Without that crisp, precise language, he had left it up to chance for the audience, in this case, a reporter, to interpret his theme or grab another of his quotes and elevate it to become the article's main message. You can't just hope your listener will piece a message together correctly.

A memorable message is intentional—it doesn't rely on interpretation or guesswork.

---

8 Tips for Calming Nerves

Deliver an Impactful Presentation and *Enjoy It at the Same Time*

"You don't rise to the level of the occasion; you fall to the level of your preparation."

—Attributed to Greek poet Archilochus (c. 680–645 BCE)

There's No Substitute for Practicing Out Loud

PREPARE TO FAIL WHEN YOU FAIL TO PREPARE.

I'm sure you've read or heard these words before but it's so true. Becoming a confident and comfortable presenter is not an intellectual exercise. It's a physical one. You can't just think about what you want to talk about. You can't just read this book. You have to *do stuff*. You have to put in the work. And yet I still have plenty of clients who tell me they spend hours and hours preparing for a presentation, but they still don't feel great when they're delivering. They don't feel great about how their content connects with their audience, and they don't feel good about how their stomach feels while they're in front of the room or on the stage talking.

As my wonderful Croatia-based managing director client, Nina, once told me, "I just want to enjoy myself at least once when I'm presenting before my employees."

I want you all to enjoy it, too. So, for this "Be It!" section, I am going to explore the steps I use and encourage my clients to use. It's a *more effective* way to prepare for your next presentation. Whether you need to present a five-minute sales update before ten of your peers or take the stage to deliver a forty-five-minute keynote address before a thousand strangers. I've done both, and I want to help you become confident and comfortable, and even enjoy yourself, too.

Remember, your self-acceptance and your self-development are living in harmony.

Mindset Prep and Nerves: Remembering You're Not Alone

Let's start by acknowledging the first thing that leaps into most people's minds when they are asked to give a presentation: "I'm nervous." I'm here to reassure you that **everyone feels nervous** before a presentation, even seasoned professionals. They really do.

A couple of years ago, I had the pleasure of meeting Dr. Wendy Suzuki at a conference I facilitated in Phoenix. She told me she considers herself an introvert, and she definitely gets nervous before she speaks. She is also the Dean of Arts and Sciences at New York University and a leading neuroscientist and spoke about how to take care of our brains. She stressed that a bit of anxiety, like when preparing or delivering a presentation, is a good thing. She then offered a fix, suggesting that even a ten-minute walk outside can give us a bubble bath of feel-good neurochemicals like dopamine and serotonin.

"Instead of letting fear hold you back, use it as rocket fuel for your goals."

—Dr. Wendy Suzuki[1]

---

8 Tips for Calming Nerves

Deliver an Impactful Presentation and *Enjoy It at the Same Time*

"You don't rise to the level of the occasion; you fall to the level of your preparation."

—Attributed to Greek poet Archilochus (c. 680–645 BCE)

There's No Substitute for Practicing Out Loud

PREPARE TO FAIL WHEN YOU FAIL TO PREPARE.

I'm sure you've read or heard these words before but it's so true. Becoming a confident and comfortable presenter is not an intellectual exercise. It's a physical one. You can't just think about what you want to talk about. You can't just read this book. You have to *do stuff.* You have to put in the work. And yet I still have plenty of clients who tell me they spend hours and hours preparing for a presentation, but they still don't feel great when they're delivering. They don't feel great about how their content connects with their audience, and they don't feel good about how their stomach feels while they're in front of the room or on the stage talking.

As my wonderful Croatia-based managing director client, Nina, once told me, "I just want to enjoy myself at least once when I'm presenting before my employees."

I want you all to enjoy it, too. So, for this "Be It!" section, I am going to explore the steps I use and encourage my clients to use. It's a *more effective* way to prepare for your next presentation. Whether you need to present a five-minute sales update before ten of your peers or take the stage to deliver a forty-five-minute keynote address before a thousand strangers. I've done both, and I want to help you become confident and comfortable, and even enjoy yourself, too.

Remember, your self-acceptance and your self-development are living in harmony.

Mindset Prep and Nerves: Remembering You're Not Alone

Let's start by acknowledging the first thing that leaps into most people's minds when they are asked to give a presentation: "I'm nervous." I'm here to reassure you that **everyone feels nervous** before a presentation, even seasoned professionals. They really do.

A couple of years ago, I had the pleasure of meeting Dr. Wendy Suzuki at a conference I facilitated in Phoenix. She told me she considers herself an introvert, and she definitely gets nervous before she speaks. She is also the Dean of Arts and Sciences at New York University and a leading neuroscientist and spoke about how to take care of our brains. She stressed that a bit of anxiety, like when preparing or delivering a presentation, is a good thing. She then offered a fix, suggesting that even a ten-minute walk outside can give us a bubble bath of feel-good neurochemicals like dopamine and serotonin.

"Instead of letting fear hold you back, use it as rocket fuel for your goals."

—Dr. Wendy Suzuki[1]

The reporter did an okay job capturing the essence of the conversation, but the message could have been much more powerful if it had been explicit. Think about it this way: a memorable message serves as the *cornerstone* of your communication. It's the specific point you want people to remember and, ideally, act on. If it's fuzzy, people will walk away with impressions, not actions.

Why a Clear, Standalone Message Is Essential

Another client of mine, a sales executive from Italy, once told me, "I don't like to prepare too carefully because I trust my audience to be smart enough to infer what I want."

But this is where many communicators misjudge the listening environment. Audiences aren't as focused on us as we might think. They may be listening, but their minds wander. They're thinking about other priorities, like an argument with a family member, or about the temperature in the room, or why they didn't wear different socks. Just like any of us, your audience is constantly dealing with mental distractions.

When you're the speaker, however, you don't feel these distractions in the same way. You know your own intent, you feel passionate about it, and you think the audience is tracking with you step by step. But in reality, they might only be partially engaged. This is why a standalone, repeatable message—something clear, brief, and resonant—is so crucial. It helps cut through all the background noise and make your point the most memorable part of their day.

Crafting Your Message: The What and the Aspirational Why

I want you to think about dividing your message into two parts: *what* you want your audience to do and *why* they will care.

The *what* is the action—be it signing onto an initiative, agreeing to a follow-up meeting, or adopting a new process. It's a clear and concrete step that is easy for them to remember and repeat.

Then there's the *why*. Why should this action matter to them? Why should they feel motivated to take it? This is where you need to connect with them emotionally. Tying your message to an aspirational benefit—the improvement it will bring to their work, their goals, or their lives—invites your audience to see themselves in the vision.

The *why* should give them a sense of purpose behind the action, one that resonates on a personal level. This blend of clarity and meaning is what makes a message memorable and persuasive.

For instance, you're rolling out a new internal mentoring program. You could say, "We're launching a mentoring initiative—please sign up by Friday." That's the *what.*

Or you could say, "We're launching a mentoring initiative to help you learn from leaders who've walked your path—and to offer your own hard-earned wisdom to someone else. Sign up by Friday, and let's build the kind of workplace where growth is contagious."

Same request, but now the *why* taps into belonging, legacy, and personal development—all things that hopefully will make people *want* to be part of the program. That's the idea of adding an aspirational *why* to go along with whatever your *what* is.

The Importance of Saying It Out Loud

Once you have your message crafted, the next essential step is to speak it out loud—over and over again. I often tell my clients that crafting a message is not just an intellectual exercise. You need to muscle-memory it into your delivery. When you say the message out loud, it becomes more than just words on a page; it becomes part of your communication style.

When you repeat it out loud, you'll also notice whether it flows easily, resonates, and feels natural to say. I advise my clients to practice this enough times that they can deliver it confidently, even under pressure. This helps embed the message in their memory, making it easier to deliver smoothly in the moment, rather than stumbling or improvising.

An Example in Practice: The Power of a Repeatable Message

A memorable message is one that the audience can repeat to themselves, even long after the meeting or talk has ended.

If they can't remember your message, they can't act on it.

I've worked with countless clients who have gone through entire meetings and then realized later that they forgot to actually state their call to action. They had to follow up with a second meeting or a phone call, or write an email to clarify the ask—losing valuable time and, in some cases, momentum and credibility.

Consider the difference in impact when a message is well crafted and delivered seamlessly. I remember working with a CEO who, in launching a new initiative, framed her message as, "Let's make every customer feel they are our only customer." That statement became a mantra within the company. Employees repeated it in meetings, used it as a guide in customer interactions, and it transformed how the organization saw customer service. A clear, repeatable message doesn't just communicate; it creates a ripple effect that permeates the organization and inspires action.

Incorporating Style: It's Okay to Be Catchy

Some clients tell me, "But I don't want it to sound like a slogan." To this, I say, if you can incorporate some rhythm, alliteration, or poetry to make the message catchier, then go for it. A catchy phrase isn't a slogan; it's the vehicle for your message. Rhythmic or poetic language is simply a way to make the message stickier, to help it resonate and stay with the audience.

For instance, another client in the healthcare industry crafted the message, "Caring is our currency." The phrase not only conveyed their organizational values but was easy to remember, share, and repeat. It became a guiding principle, giving employees a clear, actionable takeaway that went beyond words on a page. And every time they repeated it, they reinforced the importance of care in their daily interactions.

Bringing It All Together: Practice, Refine, and Reinforce

When you craft your message, think about its role as the thread that ties together every part of your presentation. Revisit it at the beginning, weave it through your main points, and bring it back in your conclusion. Repetition is essential for resonance. Every time you reinforce the message, you give your audience another opportunity to connect with it.

Finally, practice makes all the difference. Crafting a message seems easier in theory than it often is in practice. But as you consider your audience, clarify your intent, and focus on the *what* and *why*, you'll find that creating a meaningful, memorable message becomes second nature over time. When your message is both precise and infused with emotion, it resonates, motivates, and becomes the North Star for your audience to follow.

When you put in the work to consider your audience first, narrow down your intent to an immediate, clearly defined action, and then craft a strong message that's clear, repeatable, and motivating—you set the stage for meaningful connection and change. This AIM approach not only brings clarity to your communication but ensures your words have the lasting impact you envision.

Now, it's your turn. Here's an exercise to help guide you in putting AIM into action. Think about your next upcoming presentation, interview, or meeting. Put your thoughts into clarity by filling out the form below.

AIM Application

1. **Identify your audience. List as much information about them as you can.**

   ____

   ____

   ____

2. **Briefly explain your intent. What do you want your audience *to do* immediately after you're done speaking?**

   ____

   ____

   ____

3. **Write your key message for this communication event. Remember, this is not your entire presentation. In about 12–14 words, describe *what* you want your audience to do and *why* it will matter to them.**

   ____

   ____

   ____

This simple framework will help you focus and get clear on what really matters before you dive into preparing for any kind of communication—whether it's a quick catch-up with your manager, a team meeting you're leading, a company town hall, a panel discussion, or, as we'll dig into next, one of the biggest and often most nerve-wracking moments—a full-on presentation.

She's written a number of books on the subject, so please check her out. She's also a very nice person. In fact, she was kind enough to recommend to me the same coach she used to fine-tune her fully fledged TED talk (which has over ten million views) for my own smaller TEDx talk. Thank you to both Wendy and Julie Burstein for the support. I appreciate you.

I'm sharing these stories here to remind you that nerves aren't unique—they're a natural part of life. Understanding this commonality allows you to lean into it with greater ease, transforming nervous energy, as Wendy writes, into enthusiasm and drive. It's helpful to know you're part of a community of people who have faced those jitters—and overcome them. Embrace your nerves as evidence you care about the message you're about to deliver. Caring is foundational to impactful presentations.

Next time you're feeling the butterflies taking over your insides, if you don't have time for a walk outside, try these tried-and-true techniques, plus a few fresher ideas to help put you more at ease.

1. **Breathe In, Breathe Out.** Nerves often throw your breathing out of whack, leaving you feeling tense and unfocused. That's where **box breathing** comes in—a technique used by everyone from my CEO clients to Navy SEALs. Here's how: inhale for four counts, hold for four counts, exhale for four counts, and hold again for four counts. Repeat this for a minute or two. This rhythmic breathing steadies your heart rate, centers your mind, and can help slow the butterflies.

2. **Try a Power Pose.** The idea of standing tall in a power pose gained widespread popularity through Harvard researcher Amy Cuddy's famous TED talk.[2] However, it's worth noting that the technique has been somewhat controversial—subsequent studies haven't consistently replicated the dramatic effects originally claimed. That said, placebos are real, and if standing in a superhero stance for a couple of minutes makes you feel more confident, then give it a go. If it works for you, keep doing it!

3. **Picture Success.** Visualization can be an anxiety reducer. Close your eyes and imagine yourself nailing the presentation—smiling, confident, and connecting with your audience. Picture applause or nods of agreement. Focusing on this positive outcome can help shift your mindset from fear to excitement.

4. **Shake It Out.** In 2015, I was one of the warm-up speakers before self-help megastar Tony Robbins[3] took the stage at an event in Dublin. His team had placed a mini trampoline backstage so he could bounce before he went on. Along with plenty of fist-pumping, yelling, and the rock music he plays during his shows, he is clearly channeling whatever nervous energy he may have into a natural high. If you can't bring a mini trampoline with you everywhere you go, try jumping jacks, jogging in place, or shaking out your arms and legs. Like Wendy's recommended walk, any form of physical movement can release tension and also boost those endorphins before you present.
5. **Ground Yourself.** If your thoughts start to spiral, try a grounding exercise. Press your feet firmly into the floor and focus on the sensation. Or use the **5-4-3-2-1 technique**. Identify five things you see, four things you hear, three things you feel, two things you smell, and one thing you taste. The idea here is to pull yourself out of the overwhelming swirl in your head and focus instead on the present.
6. **Adopt a Pre-Show Ritual.** Create a simple pre-presentation ritual. This could be listening to a specific song, repeating an empowering mantra like "I've got this," or even sipping a favorite tea. Familiar rituals can provide a sense of control and calm.
7. **Your Strange but Effective Neuroscience Disrupter Hack.** Finally, here's a communication hack that may seem a little unusual but has proven to be incredibly effective, especially in moments of high stress or uncertainty. Whether you're surprised by a tough question or feel your nerves starting to take over before you begin to speak, this simple technique can help you regain composure quickly and confidently. When no one can see your hands, take your thumb from one hand and place it in the center of the palm of your other hand. Press firmly. Then, you can gently clasp your two hands around each other, which shields your palm-pressing thumb from anyone watching. The act is designed to remind you to maintain control over your facial expressions and tone of voice, ensuring you come across as calm and composed.

I had been recommending this technique to people for years and wasn't sure whether it was more of a placebo, so I asked my wonderful neuroscientist friend Wendy Suzuki, and she verified the move. The small physical action is more than just a distraction—it's a neuroscience-backed disruptor. It works by interrupting the emotional response triggered by the amygdala, the part of your brain responsible for processing fear and anxiety. By engaging in this action, you redirect your focus to the prefrontal cortex—the logical, decision-making center of your brain.

The next time you feel your confidence wavering or are taken by surprise, give this technique a try. It's a powerful tool to help you stay on track, keep your cool, and communicate with clarity and poise.

Above all, remember, nerves mean you are human and that you care—and that's a good thing. With these techniques, I'm confident you will be able to take more control and exude confidence to others, which, in turn, builds your own feelings of confidence.

Our thoughts don't change our actions. Our actions change our thoughts.

The Audience Factor: They're on Your Side

This might be the most nerve-reducing and empowering thought of all: **your audience wants you to succeed**. Think of it this way: they've chosen to spend time with you, eager to learn, to gain insight, and to walk away with something valuable. This investment in your success is reciprocal; the more you succeed, the more they gain from the experience.

As I outlined in Chapter 7, it's essential you keep shifting your mindset from *self-focus* to *audience-focus*. Stop thinking about scrutiny and start focusing on feeling collaborative. This is a presentation, yes, but it's also an exchange. It's about what you can give to them and the impact your words can make.

Content Creation: Crafting a Presentation with the Inverted Pyramid Approach

Whether you're asking for a raise or pitching for a five-hundred-million-dollar investment (I've advised on both), the success of your presentation comes down to three factors: strategy, structure, and delivery. Without them, even the best ideas can fall flat. My go-to system, honed over years of journalism and leadership training, is the **Inverted Pyramid Approach**.

This method, inspired by my days as a reporter, focuses on putting the most important information upfront. In journalism school, we learned to start articles with the headline and lead paragraph—what the reader needs to know immediately—and then add details in descending order of importance. This principle applies to any communication, including presentations.

The Inverted Pyramid Approach is simple: **Headline. Support. Wrap**.

Picture the Pyramid

Visualize an upside-down triangle, wide at the top and narrowing to a point. Divide it into three sections:

1. **Headline.** Your big idea at the top.
2. **Support.** The evidence, story, anecdote, or data that backs it up.
3. **Wrap.** The closing reinforcement of your message.

Here's how to structure your presentation using this model:

HEADLINE

Start with the most important point: your headline. The first moments of your presentation are critical for grabbing your audience's attention. Often, speakers lose their audience by spending precious time on context, history, or lead-up before they get to the "so what?" Instead, flip the script. Start with your big idea or the action you want your audience to take.

A strong headline is clear, confident, and positive for your listeners. For example:

- "This quarter, I've delivered fifty thousand dollars in cost savings for the company. I'd like to discuss how this contribution can be acknowledged in terms of compensation or recognition."
- "Using these techniques, you'll connect better and win more deals."

This isn't the time for a lengthy preamble—get straight to the point. When your audience knows what's at stake from the beginning, they're more likely to stay engaged.

SUPPORT

Next, support your headline with compelling evidence. This is where you bring in data, stories, anecdotes, or visuals to reinforce your message.

Tailor your support to your audience—what resonates with a board of directors will differ from what inspires your team in a staff meeting.

For instance, if your headline is about saving the company money, follow it with specifics:

- Highlight the strategies you used.
- Share an example of a successful initiative.
- Include metrics that quantify your impact.

Keep this section dynamic and flexible. If you have limited time, present just one or two supporting points. If you have more time, you can expand with additional layers of evidence, but keep it simple and focused. A good rule of thumb is to structure your support around no more than three key points, each backed by clear evidence.

This section is also where storytelling shines. A well-told story captivates your audience and makes your message more memorable.

WRAP

End with a bang by reinforcing your main takeaway. The last thing you say is often what sticks with your audience, so make it count. I have often heard people conclude what would have otherwise been a memorable and meaningful presentation with the following words:

"Well, that's all the time I have. Any questions?"

Don't make that mistake. Your audience only remembers a fraction of what you just told them. So, take advantage of the final words you say to make them really matter. Restate your headline with energy and enthusiasm. Remind your audience of the positive action you want them to take and the benefits it will bring.

For example:

- "Rewarding my efforts will incentivize even greater savings next quarter."
- "By adopting these techniques, you'll achieve stronger connections and higher wins."

This is your moment to leave them motivated, inspired, and ready to act. Your goal is to deliver your wrap-up or conclusion with even more energy than you brought to your opening.

Why the Inverted Pyramid Works

There are countless ways to structure a presentation, but I always encourage starting with the inverted pyramid. Why? Because it's simple, effective, and adaptable to any audience or scenario. By leading with your strongest point, backing it up with evidence, and closing with conviction, you ensure your message is clear and compelling, no matter how much or how little time you have to present.

So, the next time you're preparing for a high-stakes presentation, start with the *headline*, build with *support*, and close with a strong *wrap*. It's a formula that works, whether you're pitching a big idea, making a bold ask, or sharing a game-changing insight.

Bringing Your Presentation to Life Through Storytelling

The support or middle part of your presentation is the place for stories. Stories are the heart of any presentation. They captivate, connect, and make even the driest of topics come alive. Yet I've had clients tell me, "I never tell stories because I've never done anything interesting." That couldn't be further from the truth. Everyone has stories, and everyone can tell them. It's all about discovering those moments and weaving them into your presentation.

Think about it: when you insert a human, personal story into your presentation, you turn abstract concepts into relatable, memorable experiences. Even a standard business update can become a standing-ovation-worthy moment when paired with the right story.

Finding Your Story

Start by reflecting on the theme of your presentation. Identify a keyword that represents your topic. Then ask yourself, *What's the first experience that comes to mind when I think of this word?*

I once worked with a client in Prague who was preparing a high-stakes business presentation. We were exploring the power of anchoring his message with a personal story—something that could bring his keyword, "priority," to life. At first, nothing came to mind. But after a pause, a quiet smile spread across his face as he began to tell me about a moment he hadn't thought of in years.

He was working from home, deep in focus, when his three-year-old son came padding into the room, clutching a slightly battered Thomas the

Tank Engine. "Daddy, can you help me build the track?" his son asked. My client's first instinct was to wave the boy off—he was in the middle of something, after all. But another thought tugged at him. Instead of brushing his son away, he closed his laptop, sat on the floor, and gave his son his full attention for fifteen uninterrupted minutes of play.

When he finally stood up to return to work, his little boy looked up at him with grateful eyes and said, *"Thank you, Daddy. You're my best friend."*

In that simple, tender exchange, my client had found his story. A real moment that beautifully embodied the meaning of *priority*—not just as a buzzword for business, but as a conscious act of choosing what truly matters in a given moment.

Later, when he chose to share this story in his presentation, connecting it to the importance of identifying true priorities in the workplace, his audience erupted into applause, and everyone in the room stood up. A standing ovation. What could have been a standard, forgettable business update became a moment of profound human connection.

To help you craft the story once you've identified it, envision the five points on a star:

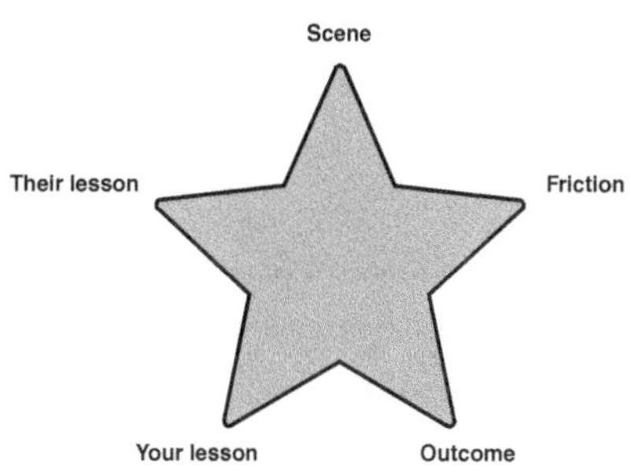

The Five Points to Star-Studded Storytelling

1. **Scene**
   Set the stage for your audience. Paint a picture that brings your story to life. Where were you? What was happening? You don't have to be wordy here, but be selective. Colors, sounds, flavors, seasons, temperatures. These matter here because they transport your listeners into your world.

For example, with my client's "priority" story:

"It was a Tuesday morning, my desk piled with reports, and my laptop buzzing with notifications when my son tugged at my sleeve, holding his train set."

2. **Challenge or Friction**

   Introduce the tension or problem. What challenge were you facing? What is the dilemma? Friction is what keeps people engaged; it's the "What happens next?"

   In the story:

   "I was torn. I had a deadline looming, but my son's hopeful eyes were hard to ignore."

3. **Outcome**

   Share how the situation was resolved. Importantly, outcomes don't have to be major victories. Disappointments or vulnerabilities can also resonate deeply with your audience.

   Here, the outcome was simple yet impactful:

   "I chose to step away for fifteen minutes. It wasn't long, but when I returned to my desk, his quiet 'Thank you, Daddy. You're my best friend,' stuck with me."

4. **Takeaway for Me**

   Explain what you learned from the experience. Why did this moment stay with you?

   For example:

   "It reminded me that while work is important, understanding what truly matters in each moment is essential."

5. **Takeaway for My Audience**

   Finally, connect the story back to your audience. This is the most critical piece. What's the broader lesson they can apply to their own lives or work?

   "My son's gratitude reminded me of the power of priorities. At work, we need to ask ourselves: what truly deserves our focus right now?"

Why Stories Work

Stories humanize us. They make our audience feel like they're not just hearing facts or data but connecting with a real person who has struggled, learned, and grown—just like them. The best part? Your story doesn't have to be extraordinary. It just has to be authentic.

So, the next time you're crafting a presentation, think about your theme, choose a keyword, and start exploring your own experiences. Remember, the most powerful moments often lie in the simplest stories—like spending fifteen minutes with a child. Tell them with heart, and you'll not only inform your audience, you'll inspire them.

Creating Your Own Star-Studded Story Structure

Take a moment to think about an upcoming business presentation, pitch, or talk you'll be giving. It could be a formal client presentation, a team meeting, or even a quick update in a cross-functional setting. Now, let's go deeper.

This exercise is designed to help you uncover a personal, human story that will bring your message to life—one that connects emotionally and makes your key point stick.

What's the Theme of Your Presentation?

____

What's a Keyword from That Theme?

____

Think of a Story Connected to That Keyword

____

Now Organize Your Thoughts into the Five Points

1. **Scene**

2. **Friction**

3. **Outcome**

4. **Lesson for You**

5. **Takeaway or Lesson for Your Audience**

Practicing Your Presentation: How to Make Every Rehearsal Count

The saying "practice makes perfect" has been passed around for decades, but let me offer you a refinement:

Practice doesn't make perfect—practice makes permanent.

So, how you practice matters as much, if not more than, how much you practice. If you rehearse without intention or strategy, you risk cementing habits that don't serve you.

Here's how to practice in ways that build confidence, clarity, and connection.

1. **Practice Out Loud, Every Time**
   I've stressed this already, and I know it might feel silly at first, but there's no substitute for practicing aloud. Simply reading over your notes or flipping through slides in your head doesn't simulate the experience of delivering to an audience. You need to hear your words, feel the rhythm, and catch moments where you stumble or struggle to transition smoothly. Oftentimes, we don't write the way we speak, and when you actually try to say the lovely, elaborate sentence you created in writing, your tongue gets twisted. When you practice out loud, you can catch these in advance and modify them. When you don't, you won't.

2. **Record Yourself on Camera**

   I've also made this recommendation before, but once again, use your phone or computer to record yourself presenting. Then watch the playback—with sound and on mute.

   - **With sound on.** Evaluate your tone, pacing, and energy. If you sound bored or disengaged, your audience will feel it too. Be honest: do you like the way you sound? If not, adjust your vocal energy. (And yes, this is hard and can feel embarrassing, even in a room by yourself. Do it anyway, you'll thank me later. It's easier the more you do it.)
   - **With sound off.** Focus on your body language and facial expressions. Are you animated and confident? Or do you seem stiff, disengaged, or overly fidgety?

   Imagine you're the audience. **Would you enjoy watching yourself?** If the answer is no, that's your cue to adjust.

If you think your presentation feels boring, imagine how your audience feels.

---

3. **Don't Memorize Everything**

   Memorizing an entire script often backfires. If you lose your place or forget a line, you'll panic and that throws off your flow. Instead, focus on understanding your presentation's structure:

   - Know your main sections and the logical order they follow.
   - Memorize key phrases or power statements that you can sprinkle throughout. These are your standout lines, the ones you want your audience to remember.

   What should you memorize? **Your opening and closing**. The introduction sets the tone, and the conclusion leaves the audience with their final impression of you and your topic. Both deserve extra attention.

4. **Practice in Reverse**

   Many presenters spend the majority of their rehearsal time perfecting their introduction. While that's important, it often leaves the conclusion under-rehearsed. And remember, your conclusion is **critical**: it's the final energy and message you leave with your audience.

Flip your practice order:

- Start by rehearsing the conclusion until you can deliver it confidently and with energy.
- Then, move on to the middle sections, working backward toward the introduction.

This ensures that every part of your presentation gets equal attention.

5. **Rehearse with a Live Audience**

   Ask a friend, family member, or colleague to watch you practice. A live audience can give you feedback on areas where you're unclear, disengaged, or need more energy. They can also point out parts they find particularly compelling, helping you refine your strengths. Choose someone who will give you honest, constructive feedback—not just compliments.

6. **Focus on Delivery, Not Just Content**

   When you're presenting, your delivery is as important as your words. Here are some techniques to enhance it:

   - **Energy.** If you feel your energy dipping, your audience's will dip too. Punch up your enthusiasm, even if it feels a little over the top. I promise you, unless you're being extremely theatrical, heightened energy (aligned with the tone of the subject, of course) will be well received by most audiences.
   - **Speed.** Avoid speaking too fast due to nerves. Use natural pauses to emphasize key points and give your audience time to process.
   - **Eye contact.** Practice looking at different parts of the room, even if you're rehearsing alone. Imagine connecting with individual audience members.

7. **Watch for the Boring Factor**

   If a section of your presentation feels boring to you while you rehearse, it will absolutely feel boring to your audience. Rewrite or reframe that part to inject more energy, a story, or a compelling statistic. Your enthusiasm for the material is contagious—if you're engaged, your audience will be too.

8. **Evaluate and Refine After Each Practice**

   Treat each rehearsal like a mini performance. Afterward, ask yourself:

   - What worked well?

- Where did I feel unsure or lose my place?
- Did my delivery feel natural and confident?

Refine your approach based on what you observe. The more you tweak and improve, the more polished you'll feel. How many times should you rehearse? I get asked this a lot, and there's no fixed number of hours that you must dedicate. Some people are quicker studies or have had more experience, so they'll need less time. The key is to get comfortable delivering the material. Practice as you want to perform.

Death By PowerPoint Continues

A few words about putting too many words on your slide deck. When you're presenting, your PowerPoint slides or visuals should serve as your backup singers—not the main act. You are the presentation. Your presence, your voice, your delivery—that's what your audience connects with. Slides are there to support your story, not steal the spotlight. If they're overloaded or packed with dense content, they end up competing with you. Instead of listening to what you're saying, your audience is reading ahead, getting distracted, or zoning out entirely.

The whole idea behind using fewer slides—an approach many organizations encourage—is not to cram all your information onto one or two mega-slides. But that's what often happens. A slide gets overloaded with twenty-five bullet points and is flashed up, and while you're talking about the first point, your audience is off reading bullet number eighteen. You've lost the narrative.

Remember, you're not there to show a book on the wall—you're there to be the movie.

Be the movie.
Not the book.

Give your audience a visual that supports what you're saying right now. I'd rather you run through more slides with fewer words and charts on them. Keep it simple, clear, and aligned with your message. That way, your slides enhance your story instead of hijacking it. Don't be *that* person who kicks off a slide by saying, "Sorry, I know this is a busy slide." If you have to apologize for it, it probably shouldn't be on the screen.

If your audience needs a microscope to follow along, you're not helping them, you're losing them. Keep it clean, keep it clear, and let your *talking* do the heavy lifting.

The Final Run

Before the big day, do at least one full rehearsal where you run through the presentation from start to finish as if it's the real thing. Use your slides, props, or notes just as you would during the actual presentation. This helps you catch any last-minute issues and boosts your confidence. If you've given yourself enough lead time for preparation before the big day, I don't recommend over-practicing the day of the event, as this can add to those nerves and stress we already discussed.

Remember, the goal of practice isn't perfection—it's preparation. When you rehearse strategically and intentionally, you'll walk into your presentation with the skills and confidence needed to deliver your message with impact.

Rehearse with purpose, and you'll walk in ready to deliver with confidence and impact.

The Big Day: Delivering the Actual Presentation

So now, let's walk into that meeting room or onto that stage. Your nerves are (relatively) calm, you have crafted compelling content complete with a couple of human stories or anecdotes, and you have practiced aloud—not to perfection, but to a realistic level of comfort.

Let's make sure you deliver in poise and confidence to best connect with your audience. Let's *amplify* who you are dedicating yourself to become.

Wardrobe Choice: Dress to Complement, Not Distract

Please select your outfit at least the night before your presentation. Don't just envision what you will wear. Take the clothing out of your closet and examine your chosen outfit. Any loose buttons? Does something need to be pressed? Try everything on. Does everything still fit?

You want to be confident and comfortable in your clothing. **What you wear can be as telling as what you say.** Clothing, especially in a professional setting, signals the respect and attention you bring to your presentation. In Chapter 6, we delved into classic wardrobe choices for their versatility and timeless appeal. Here's how those lessons apply to public speaking:

- **Be Intentional.** Dressing in a polished, professional way that feels authentic to you projects confidence. That confidence translates to your audience, helping to create a positive impression before you even speak.
- **Avoid Distractions.** Choose attire that complements your message. Avoid unflattering colors or patterns that may detract from your words. Simplicity in clothing can focus the audience's attention on your message, not your outfit.
- **Leverage Subtle Power Cues.** Classic pieces like a blazer or fitted shirt can subtly convey authority. Consider adding an accessory that aligns with your brand (a single piece, like a watch or necklace, can convey reliability and a touch of personality).

Your On-Stage Body Language Advantage: Projecting Confidence and Connection

We touched on gestures and postures in Chapter 3, and it's worth repeating here: body language is one of your most powerful communication tools. Your posture, gestures, and facial expressions tell a story long before you say a word.

When you take the stage, your nonverbal cues can build trust and engagement or erode them. Here are essential body-language elements to keep in mind:

- **Start Strong.** Even before you take the stage, make sure your posture and gait are activated. When you walk on stage, I want you to stride with purpose. Don't shuffle or slouch. Believe me, I've seen both. Enter with a posture of confidence—core engaged, shoulders back. This not only projects strength to your audience but reinforces your confidence in yourself. Some conferences will offer walk-on music.

Pick something appropriately upbeat. Show energy immediately as you're going up the stairs to the stage.

- **Establish Eye Contact.** Connect with different people throughout the room. Eye contact shows you're not just presenting *at* them but *with* them.
- **Use Open Gestures.** Avoid crossing your arms, keeping your hands relaxed and open to convey openness and trust. Hand gestures can emphasize your points when used thoughtfully, but avoid overdoing it. Keep away from the podium unless you absolutely need it.

The Power of "The Pleasantries"

Too many presenters rush into their content the moment they take the stage, diving headfirst into their slides or script. While enthusiasm is important, skipping a proper introduction can leave both you and your audience feeling a bit unsteady. That's where the power of what I describe as "the pleasantries" comes in.

Think of *the pleasantries* as an airplane's runway—a moment to steady yourself before taking off. Taking time to express a few pleasantries allows you to:

1. **Calibrate your voice to the room's acoustics.**
2. **Find your stance and ground yourself.**
3. **Connect with your audience on a human level before jumping into the heart of your message.**

It's the connection before the content.

Your pleasantry can be as simple as a warm greeting:

- **"Good morning. It's great to be here with you all today."**
- **"I hope you're as excited about this session as I am."**

Alternatively, depending on your subject and setting, you might expand it into a brief icebreaker or personal anecdote. For instance, if you're speaking at a leadership summit, you could say:

- **"It's a privilege to join such a dynamic group of leaders today. I've already overheard some inspiring conversations during the coffee break!"**

This small effort serves two purposes:

For you—it creates a moment to breathe, center yourself, and get comfortable looking out at your audience.

For your audience—it sets a friendly tone, helping them warm up to you and feel engaged from the start.

Whether it's a simple hello or a longer opening thought, don't underestimate the power of the pleasantry. It's a small investment of time with a big payoff: a smoother start, a more comfortable connection, and a confident springboard into your presentation.

Congratulations! You've Successfully Presented! Now a Quick Word about Q&A

Handling a question-and-answer (Q&A) session with grace and confidence is a critical skill for any presenter. While most audience members have positive motivations, occasionally, you'll face questions that are challenging, hostile, or simply off-topic. To navigate these moments, I recommend three simple techniques: The Park, The Unpack, and The Pivot.

1. **The Park**
   This approach is perfect for questions requiring more time or context to answer, or for those that are off-topic or inappropriate. Be honest and realistic, acknowledging the question and providing a timeline for follow-up if needed. For example, say:

   > *"That's an important question, and I want to ensure I give you an accurate answer. Let me research this further, and I'll get back to you by* [specific time]*."*

   Alternatively, if the question veers off topic, respectfully suggest taking it offline:

   > *"I'd love to discuss this with you in more detail after the session."*

   This keeps the conversation focused and professional.

2. **The Unpack**
   When faced with a complicated or multi-part question, use this technique to clarify, gain time, or redirect the asker's thoughts. Invite them to break it down with prompts like:

   > *"Can you give me an example of what you mean?"*
   >
   > *"Which part of your question is most important to address first?"*
   >
   > *"Can you expand on that?"*

This not only gives you time to think on your feet but also ensures you're addressing the question effectively.

3. **The Pivot**

   Sometimes, a question needs an acknowledgment before moving to a different point you'd rather reinforce. Use the word *and* instead of *but* to maintain a positive tone. For instance:

   "That's an interesting perspective, and it ties into the main takeaway I'd like to highlight, which is..."

   This subtle shift allows you to control the narrative *without* dismissing the question.

   By mastering these techniques, you'll handle Q&A sessions with confidence, leaving your audience impressed by your professionalism and composure.

The Confidence Loop

Remember, presentations are not merely to inform, they're about connecting, building confidence, and sharing value. Your wardrobe choices, body language, preparation, and mindset combine alongside your authoritative delivery to create a meaningful and memorable experience for your audience—and for you.

After you've finished and had a chance to relax, reflect, and journal, capture a few things that could have gone better. But mostly focus on what went well. Every positive aspect that you are now doing with more purpose is a victory, and I want you to savor each one, even if you experience a minor setback like the unexpected technical difficulty of the microphone not working or the slides advancing too quickly. It's okay. It's happened to most of us. If you forgot a word or two, don't worry about it. Your audience doesn't know what you *intended* to say; they only know what you said. You'll be better next time, and you'll learn something else.

Developing this skill takes time, so be kind to yourself.

Speaking of taking time, it was about three months from when we first began working together on improving not only her presentation abilities but also her feelings toward the experience, when I received an excited Zoom call from my client from Croatia.

"It happened; it really happened!" Nina exclaimed. "I told stories, leaned into my human experience, and even looked into the eyes of my audience. I actually *enjoyed* giving a presentation." Hooray for Nina!

You will come to be good at it and love it too.

Next up, I have a few more *amplify* applications to explore with you. If you've ever flubbed an interview, forgotten to actually *ask* for the pay raise during your meeting, or struggled with a difficult conversation, Chapter 9 is for you. See you there.

9 The Interview

Clarity Under Pressure

> "I don't always think of the perfect answer in an interview.
> But when I do, it's always fifteen minutes after I've left."
> —Often attributed to Mark Twain

Help Them Imagine You in Your Dream Role

AT SOME POINT, WE ALL GO THROUGH AN INTERVIEW PROCESS.

That out-of-body experience where you find yourself sitting on one side of a desk or table, and the person who may or may not hire you is seated opposite. Perhaps you're meeting virtually on Zoom or Teams. Whether it's in person or remote, this experience is pressure-filled. Every week, I meet new people as I try to continue developing my business. I connect with leaders on LinkedIn and invite them to a virtual coffee. But it's essentially a mini-interview. I want them to like me. To believe that my expertise can help them or their employees become better versions of themselves. I want them to imagine me working with their companies, and I want them to hire me.

We're all constantly interviewing throughout our lives. New jobs. New relationships. New places to live. We can learn from each new experience and become better, or not.

Mastering the Interview Process

The interview is not merely about answering questions—it's about crafting and delivering a compelling story of who you are, what drives you, and why you're the perfect fit for the role. It's your opportunity to *amplify* you. To showcase control over your words, body language, and voice, enhancing your presence and influence in a high-stakes setting. When you're aiming for a new job or promotion, preparation, practice, and follow-up are critical to success.

Starting with You: Crafting Your "Tight Is Right" Personal Story

When the interviewer asks, "Tell me about yourself," they're not looking for a recitation of your résumé or CV. They want to hear something short and sweet—a tight, engaging story that conveys who you are, what drives you, and what you're passionate about. I know we've all heard about the elevator pitch. That used to be about being able to deliver a personal description of yourself in thirty seconds—about the time it would take an elevator to move from one floor to the next. To be really effective, it should be even quicker.

For most of us, this doesn't come naturally.

After I moved to Ireland, people never failed to ask, "What brought you here?" It's embarrassing to admit that I used to drone on: *"Well, actually, it was my now ex-husband's decision to move us here and, at that time, our marriage had been slowly unraveling for years like a badly knit sweater and pretty much the moment we landed I realized I needed to go back to the United States to divorce him properly then turn right around and return to Ireland because the people here are so welcoming and the air felt fresher and I figured I could build my business and find a great school for my daughter and yada-yada-yada blah blah blah..."*

Nobody wants to listen to a rambling sob story like that from some random person they just met at a networking event, do they? "Okay, lady, nice to meet you. Uhm, I've got to go."

So, I realized pretty quickly I needed to craft a simple answer which was true, of course, but didn't go into too much complicated and overly personal detail.

I moved to Ireland because it's a great place to do business and it's a safe place to raise my daughter.

That's the line I came up with. I can assure you it took me a lot longer to craft that than it did just now for you to read it. I feel confident it now hits the mark. The sentiments are true without going into unnecessary detail. It sounds conversational and natural when I deliver it. And the bonus is that it's also uplifting toward the Irish person who asks me the question, because I've just given their country a couple of compliments.

The answer *amplifies* me rather than *depletes* my credibility or impact, and it quickly moves the conversation to the other person.

The same approach will help you in interviews, networking events, and so on.

Here's my framework to help you organize your thoughts. I've even given you some lines after each bulleted element to help you begin crafting your own opening description.

You can always revise your answers. But do take some time here to begin gathering your thoughts. Don't aim for perfection when you start writing below.

- **Begin with Your Core Values.** Share what drives you professionally and personally. For example, your first draft might be, "I'm deeply motivated by solving complex challenges and creating systems that help teams perform at their best." Or here's a simpler version, "I'm passionate about processes, but I don't forget the people who make them happen." Think about what drives you, and craft an opening line the same way you would for a presentation. This doesn't have to be cheesy, but do craft something tight, so you don't flounder all over the place when you get asked the question, "Tell me about yourself." Because, like with me when I moved to Ireland, you will be asked this all the time.

  ____

  ____

  ____

  ____

- **Weave in Key Achievements.** Next, highlight one or two accomplishments that align with your passion and the role, but frame them as evidence of your values. For example, "In my previous role, I led a cross-functional team to streamline operations, reducing project timelines by twenty percent. It wasn't just about efficiency—it was about building trust and collaboration among stakeholders." Spotlight two or three accomplishments and remember to add why it should matter to them. Don't recite your entire life's history. You want to keep them interested, not put them to sleep. Try to write something here.

____

____

____

- **End with Forward Focus.** As I mentioned with your achievements, don't forget to link everything back to the person on the other side of the desk or screen. Tie your story to the position you're interviewing for. For instance, "This is why I'm excited about this opportunity—it's a chance to bring my collaborative approach (or whatever characteristic or skill you are highlighting here) to a team that values innovation and impact." Now you try it:

____

____

____

As you already know, because you've been with me this far in the book, your answers should feel authentic, not rehearsed. Practice enough to ensure fluidity but leave room for genuine engagement.

The Deeper Dive into Why This Job? What More Do You Bring?

After you get through your opening lines around "Tell me about yourself," you are likely going to need to go in for a deeper dive to demonstrate what you know about the job you are seeking, and provide more insights into what you can bring to the role.

There's no workaround here, folks. You need to put in some time on each of these. Again, I've given you some blank lines to help you make notes if you'd like.

- **Research the Company.** Google the organization and read up beyond the company's website to try and absorb its values, recent achievements, challenges, and goals. Align your answers with this context. For example, "I admire how your company prioritizes sustainability, and I'm excited about contributing to your (fill in the blank) initiative to reduce environmental impact." If this sounds obvious to you, I assure you it's not!

  ____

  ____

  ____

My friend Dave Pliler has a brilliant—and painfully real—story that drives home the importance of doing a little research before a job interview. He and his wife, Kathy, own a wellness spa called *Prime IV Hydration & Wellness* in Utah. It's a growing franchise, and they were recently hiring two registered nurses—qualified professionals, mind you—for their spa.

Before the interview process began, Dave said to Kathy, "Look, if anyone comes in and tells you they actually visited a Prime IV—just walked through the door to see how we operate, what we offer—I'd hire them on the spot. If someone tells you they paid for a treatment just to experience it for themselves? Make them assistant manager."

Seems reasonable, right?

But out of twenty-five candidates, *not one* had visited a Prime IV location. Zero. Only *five* had even bothered to Google the business. The rest sat down during their interviews and—get this—actually said, "I really don't know much about what you do."

Dave just shook his head. This isn't about having a master's in business. It's about curiosity, initiative, and a basic level of care for the job you're applying for. Doing your homework shows respect—for the employer, the opportunity, and yourself.

So, if you've ever wondered whether researching the company you're applying to is really worth the time, the answer is definitely yes.

- **Research the Division.** If you're going for growth and applying for a promotion into a different department within your existing company, you can *still* do some research. Ask around. What projects are they working on? Do they have an internal awareness campaign going on that you can learn more about? Demonstrate you've made an extra effort.

___

___

___

- **Highlight Examples of Value You Can Bring.** In addition to your opening line, select three mini case studies that you are proud of or learned from. "In 2020, during Covid times, I began a rotating personal check-in program among my team members that we continue to this day, even though we are all now back in the office. We're convinced that our increased support efforts have also increased our sales numbers, which climb year after year." Each mini case study should illustrate a unique takeaway for your audience. And note, you don't necessarily need to tick through each of them in rapid succession if you are given the opportunity. I encourage you to provide one and then tell the interviewer you have a couple more, "Would you like me to share them with you?" If they say, "Sure," then go for it. But asking for their permission first allows them to give you a further invitation or move on to another line of questioning. Leave them wanting more, not losing the will to live.

___

___

___

As always, please rehearse your mini case stories *aloud* to ensure confidence and clarity.

Preparation: Crafting Your Key Messages and Questions

Create Your Own Tagline

As I've already said, your tight responses should emphasize clarity and impact. Write down the key points you want to convey and practice condensing them into succinct, memorable phrases.

For example:

- Instead of "I've worked in multiple roles, each helping me gain more skills."
- Try "*I thrive on growth*, and every role I've taken has built the expertise I now bring to this opportunity."

The first is pretty straightforward, and while factual, it is also a little routine and flat. The second uses enriched word choice and brings more motivating and upbeat emotion to the same idea. "I thrive on growth" is a power phrase. It's like your own strapline or tagline. Once you get the hang of creating and delivering these, you can sprinkle them into your conversations like cinnamon on a latte. Get it? Now, you try.

Here's a factual line about me:

____

____

Here's the same fact, but with more powered-up word choice:

____

____

Preparing Questions

It is essential that you show your interest and engagement by asking thoughtful questions back to your interviewer that reflect your research. Imagine your conversation like a tennis match. You want to land the conversation ball back into their court as many times as you can. Just like perfecting your tennis serve, crafting questions takes effort and practice. Avoid generic queries: "What's the company culture like?" Instead, aim for something more specific:

- "What does success look like in this role during the first six months?"
- "How do you see this department contributing to the company's long-term strategy?"

These questions demonstrate your understanding of the company's goals and your intention to contribute meaningfully.

The Role of Practice

Practice Out Loud

I know I've pounded on this a lot, but to effectively *amplify* your impact when you are speaking, you need to exercise the connection between your brain and your mouth. Thinking is not the same as speaking. You must exercise your voice, lips, and tongue! Speaking aloud helps you refine your tone, pacing, and emphasis. So, since we're here together in the interview chapter, I'll remind you again.

Rehearse your prepared answers to common questions in front of a mirror, record yourself, or enlist a friend for mock interviews. Listen for those pesky filler words, or a monotone delivery, or a rushed response. Adjust accordingly. Practice again. If you haven't interviewed for a while or gone to a networking event for a few months, run through your previously prepared lines again. You've probably gotten a bit rusty. It's a rinse-and-repeat process that most never take the time to do. If you do it, you amplify yourself and set yourself apart.

Amplified people get the roles.
Amplified people get what they want.

Simulate the Interview Environment If the interview is virtual, practice in your chosen setup. If it's in person, rehearse walking into the room, introducing yourself, and sitting comfortably.

Presenting Yourself: Words, Body Language, and Voice

Appearance: Dressing for Impact Your outfit should be professional, polished, and appropriate for the company culture, while reflecting your personality. Consider:

- **Neutral Options.** Opt for tailored blazers, classic button-down shirts, and neutral-colored trousers or skirts.
- **Affordable and Timeless.** Prioritize fit and quality over labels. Brands with budget-friendly professional wear are a great resource.

- **Accessories.** Keep them minimal and understated to avoid distractions.

Body Language: As I've already stressed, don't forget that your body speaks volumes before you say a word.

- **Entering the Room.** Walk confidently, make eye contact, and offer a firm (but not crushing) handshake.
- **Sitting.** Sit upright but relaxed, leaning in slightly (about thirty degrees) to show attentiveness. Keep your hands visible, resting on the table or your lap.
- **Expression.** Smile genuinely at appropriate moments. Your face should reflect engagement, openness, and interest.

For virtual interviews:

- **Set the Scene.** Ensure a clean, uncluttered background with good lighting. Position the camera at eye level.
- **On-Screen Presence.** Look directly into the camera when speaking to simulate eye contact and maintain good posture.

Voice and Speech: Your voice conveys confidence and authority.

- **Pace.** Speak clearly and at a moderate pace. Avoid rushing, even if you're nervous.
- **Tone.** Vary your pitch to emphasize key points and maintain listener engagement.
- **Energy.** Infuse enthusiasm into your responses—your passion should be evident in your delivery.

The Interview Itself: Connecting Through Rapport

Building Rapport: Connection is key to standing out. Start by thanking the interviewer for the opportunity and finding a genuine point of connection. For example:

- "Thank you for inviting me to speak with you today. I've been impressed by [specific company achievement] and am excited to learn more about how this role contributes to your mission."

Active Listening: Demonstrate that you're fully present:

- **Focus on Their Words.** Avoid formulating responses while they're speaking.
- **Acknowledge Key Points.** Paraphrase or reflect back what they've said. "It sounds like adaptability is crucial in this role—can you share an example of how the team has approached that in the past?"

Closing with Confidence: End on a strong note by reiterating your enthusiasm and fit for the role:

- "I'm truly excited about the opportunity to bring my [specific skills or values] to this role and contribute to [specific company goal]. Thank you for this conversation—I look forward to the possibility of working together."

Following Up: Sustaining the Connection

After the interview, follow up promptly:

- **Thank-You Email.** Express appreciation and reference a specific point from the conversation.
- **LinkedIn Connection.** If appropriate, connect with the interviewer and thank them again for their time.

For example:

> "Thank you for sharing insights into [specific aspect of the role]. Our conversation confirmed my excitement about contributing to [specific goal]. I'd love to stay connected."

After the Outcome: Owning Your Growth

If You Get the Job

- **Onboarding.** Prepare for your first ninety days by researching the company further, understanding team dynamics, and setting clear goals.
- **Relationships.** Build trust by actively listening to colleagues, contributing thoughtfully in meetings, and demonstrating humility.

If You Don't Get the Job

- **Seek Feedback.** Politely ask for insights into why you weren't selected. "Thank you for considering me for this role. I'd appreciate any feedback you could share to help me grow."
- **Reflect.** Use the experience to refine your approach for future opportunities.

Long-Term Brand-Building

Regardless of the outcome, view the process as part of your larger journey in shaping your professional identity.

- **Reputation.** Cultivate a reputation for professionalism, curiosity, and adaptability.
- **Networking.** Stay in touch with connections made during the interview process.
- **Continuous Development.** Invest in ongoing skill-building, from public speaking to leadership training.

By applying these techniques—preparing thoroughly, practicing deliberately, and presenting authentically—you'll not only excel in interviews but also *amplify* your overall impact, paving the way for long-term career success.

Let me share a few real-life examples.

Starting with Your Story: Who Are You?

Rosa is an engineer who wanted a promotion within her company. Rosa knew her technical expertise was solid, but she also realized that technical skills alone wouldn't win her the leadership role she sought. Together, we mapped out her strategy, from crafting a compelling narrative to practicing her delivery. When I first met Rosa, she was frustrated. "I've been at this company for ten years," she told me, "but I feel invisible when it comes to promotions." Rosa had spent so much time focused on her work she hadn't considered how to present herself effectively.

We began with the question, "Tell me about yourself." This common interview prompt can trip up even the most experienced professionals. Rosa initially responded with a laundry list of her technical qualifications. "That's not who you are," I said. "That's what you've done." Together, we reframed her answer:

- **Core Values.** Rosa reflected on her passion for problem-solving and collaboration. She shared how growing up in a small town had helped her learn to fix things herself, and she loved the challenge of finding creative solutions.
- **Key Achievements.** She highlighted her leadership in a company-wide project that reduced production delays by thirty percent, emphasizing not just the numbers but how she brought the team together to achieve them.
- **Forward Focus.** Finally, she tied her story to the leadership role she was pursuing: "I'm excited about the opportunity to lead our engineering team because I know how to bring people together to solve tough challenges."

Rosa practiced this narrative until it felt natural. When her interview came, she delivered it with confidence, leaving the panel with a clear sense of who she was and why she was the right person for the job.

Why This Job? What Do You Bring?

Let's shift to Hans, a senior vice president at a multinational organization. Hans was being considered for the global CMO role but faced stiff competition. He needed to articulate not only why he wanted the job but also what made him uniquely qualified.

When we spoke, Hans admitted he struggled with self-promotion. "I don't want to come across as arrogant," he said. This is a common concern, but it's important to remember that presenting your strengths isn't bragging—it's about clarity.

We worked together to craft a response that balanced confidence with humility:

- Hans highlighted his ability to innovate in processes, sharing how he introduced a customer feedback loop that increased retention by fifteen percent.
- He emphasized his focus on people, explaining how he built a diverse marketing team that had won multiple industry awards.
- Finally, he connected these achievements to the CMO role: "I believe the combination of innovative thinking and team leadership I've cultivated aligns perfectly with the vision for this position."

Hans practiced his responses aloud, refining his delivery to sound conversational yet impactful. When he delivered his presentation to the board, they saw not just his accomplishments, but also his passion and strategic vision.

Preparation: Words and Questions

Whether you're preparing for an interview, presentation, or pitch, preparation is non-negotiable. Consider Clara, a finance director at a growing tech company. Clara was preparing for a promotion to CFO, a role that required not only technical expertise but also strong communication skills. Clara and

I began by identifying the key messages she wanted to convey. She wrote them down:

- Her proven track record in financial strategy.
- Her ability to mentor and grow high-performing teams.
- Her vision for the company's financial future.

We then worked on crafting questions to show her interest in the role:

- "How do you see the CFO contributing to the company's long-term goals?"
- "What are the biggest challenges facing the finance team, and how can this role address them?"

Clara practiced these questions alongside her responses, ensuring she could weave them into a natural conversation. By the time her interview came, she was ready to engage confidently and thoughtfully.

Practice Makes Impact

Practicing aloud is a game-changer, and I saw this firsthand with Edward, a director at a global engineering firm. Edward was known for his technical knowledge but often struggled to articulate his ideas clearly in high-pressure situations.

We set up mock interviews, where Edward practiced answering questions in front of a mirror and recording himself. At first, he noticed filler words like "um" and "you know."Through deliberate practice, he learned to pause instead, giving himself time to think and respond with clarity.

When Edward's interview for a vice president's role arrived, his preparation paid off. His responses were polished yet genuine, and he delivered a compelling closing statement that underscored his readiness for the role.

Presenting Yourself: Wardrobe, Body Language, and Voice

Appearance: Dressing for Impact Choosing the right outfit is about more than looking polished—it's about feeling confident. Rosa, for example, initially underestimated the importance of wardrobe. "I'll just wear my usual black pantsuit," she said. But we talked about how small tweaks could elevate her look without breaking the bank.

- **For Women and Men.** A tailored blazer and well-fitting trousers or skirt in neutral colors like navy, gray, or black create a professional yet approachable impression.
- **Affordable Yet Classic.** Rosa found a chic blazer and blouse at a department store sale, proving you don't need to spend a fortune to look sharp.

Hans, on the other hand, wanted to convey authority without appearing unapproachable. He opted for a charcoal gray suit with a subtle pinstripe, paired with a crisp white shirt and a tie in a muted color.

Body Language: When I worked with Clara, we focused on her posture and gestures. She practiced sitting upright with a slight forward lean, conveying attentiveness. She also learned to keep her hands visible and relaxed, avoiding fidgeting.

Hans practiced his handshake—a firm but not crushing grip—and developed the habit of maintaining steady eye contact during conversations. For virtual settings, we ensured his camera was at eye level, and his lighting highlighted his face without casting shadows.

Voice Energy: Edward struggled with a flat, monotone voice that made his ideas seem less engaging. Together, we worked on varying his pitch and emphasizing keywords. He practiced reading aloud from scripts, exaggerating his tone at first to develop vocal energy. By the time of his interview, his voice was dynamic, holding the attention of his audience.

The Interview: Building Rapport

Building rapport is essential, as I saw with Maya, a marketing manager interviewing for a director role. Maya started her interview by thanking the panel and referencing a recent company achievement: "I'm excited to be here today. I was inspired by your recent campaign on sustainability—it's the kind of innovative work I'd love to contribute to."

Throughout the interview, Maya leaned into active listening, nodding slightly and paraphrasing key points. Her thoughtful responses and genuine curiosity made her stand out as a candidate who understood and valued the company's goals.

Closing with Confidence: Rosa practiced her closing statement multiple times, ensuring it was concise and memorable:

> "Thank you for this opportunity. I'm excited about the chance to bring my problem-solving skills and collaborative approach to this role. I believe I can make a real impact here, and I look forward to the possibility of contributing to your team."

Her interviewers left with a clear, positive impression of her readiness for leadership.

Following Up: Sustaining Connections

After his interview, Hans sent a thoughtful thank-you email, referencing a specific topic he had discussed: "I appreciated your insights on the challenges facing the marketing team. Our conversation reinforced my excitement about contributing to solutions in this role."

He also connected with the panel members on LinkedIn, adding a brief personal note. These follow-ups reinforced his professionalism and interest.

After the Outcome: Building Your Brand

If You Get the Job Rosa approached her new leadership role with the same intentionality she brought to her interview. She scheduled one-on-one meetings with her team members, asking open-ended questions to build rapport and understand their needs.

If You Don't Get the Job Maya didn't get the director role she applied for, but she didn't let that stop her. She sought feedback, using it to refine her approach for future opportunities. "I realized I needed to emphasize my leadership experience more," she shared.

Long-Term Impact: Edward, now a vice president, continues to practice his communication skills, understanding that executive presence is an ongoing journey.

Rosa has become a mentor to younger engineers, helping them navigate their own career paths.

These stories demonstrate that *amplifying* your impact isn't about perfection—it's about preparation, authenticity, and continuous growth. No matter the outcome, the lessons you learn and the connections you make are investments in your long-term success.

By mastering your words, body language, and voice, you take control of how the world sees you. And that is the foundation for a career—and life—of influence and impact. You simply cannot afford to *not* amplify yourself. ChatGPT can't speak for you—yet. And that's what my next chapter is all about. Why you must human up in this AI world.

10 Human Up in an AI World

Your Human Advantage

"The danger is that if we invest too much in developing AI and too little in developing human consciousness, the very sophisticated artificial intelligence... might only serve to empower the natural stupidity of humans."

—Yuval Harari, *21 Lessons for the 21st Century*

When a Strategy Takes Twenty Seconds

"I NEARLY FELL OFF MY CHAIR."

That's how my client, the Chief Information Officer for a global beverage brand based in Paris (you can guess which one), reflected on his day to me during one of our coaching sessions. "I typed in a prompt for a five-year marketing strategy," he went on, "and in twenty seconds, AI delivered a plan that looked eerily similar to the one my senior marketing team had spent a full month sweating over."

He laughed as he told me, but it was an uneasy kind of laugh. The kind that says, *Can you believe this?* And also says, *What does it mean for me?* Think about what he experienced: four weeks of human effort condensed into twenty seconds of machine output. His team had poured themselves into meetings, pulled late nights, debated brand positioning, and crafted and re-crafted language. Probably hundreds of hours among them. And yet, a chatbot had produced something similar in less time than it took you to read the few sentences in this chapter so far.

"I couldn't decide if I should be impressed or depressed," he admitted.

That client's experience was over a year ago from the time I'm writing this in 2025. And that tension—the tug between amazement and anxiety—is the reality many of you are likely facing right now. AI dazzles with speed, but it also pokes at an unsettling question:

If a machine can do in seconds what we do in weeks, where is our value?

The Colleague You Never Hired

AI is no longer a toy we test on the side. It's that colleague you never hired but who's suddenly everywhere. Marketing teams draft campaigns with it. HR taps it for onboarding guides. Executives lean on it for speeches, memos, even LinkedIn posts. Need a press release? Ask AI. Stuck on a tricky client email? There's a bot for that. Looking to update your CV or resume? Just attach your old one to ChatGPT to get a refreshed narrative. Want a rousing message for the next all-hands meeting? A few prompts and voilà.

The convenience is seductive. The speed feels like magic. But the more we default to it, the more inseparable from us it becomes—and the easier it is to forget what communication actually is. Communication isn't just words on a page. It's the experience you provide when you deliver it aloud. In person. It's the feeling you create—*or don't create*—for the audience on the other end. It's the connection that happens—*or doesn't*—between two real humans.

Creating a real connection is the part no machine can do for you.

A Warning We Shouldn't Ignore

Harari's warning from the start of this chapter resonates. If we over-invest in AI while under-investing in human growth, we risk empowering not intelligence, but emptiness. I don't believe people are "naturally stupid" as he states. Far from it. But I do believe that if we don't actively develop and amplify our uniquely human skills—empathy, creativity, presence—AI won't just replace tasks. It will erode the very qualities that make each of us worth connecting with.

At a four-day executive MBA conference in Louisville, Kentucky, where I was a featured speaker, I recently shared the stage with Professor Ernest O'Boyle from Indiana University's Kelley School of Business. His research focus is the future of work in an AI world. During his speech, which skills do you think he emphasized as the most important for us to be skilling up on these days? Not coding. Not data crunching. Not prompt engineering. He pointed to **empathy, collaboration, and authentic communication** as the differentiators that will matter most. In his words, the leaders who will thrive are those "who can listen deeply, work effectively with others, and communicate authentically." His academic case reinforces my practical coaching reality: the future belongs not to those who outsource their voice, but to those who *amplify* their humanity. That's what this book is all about, folks. You *can* and you *must* take more control of how you show up.

Now join me for a few stories of those who have—and sadly those who have not.

The Disappearing Leader

"Ethan" is the name I'm giving to a leader I coached recently. A director of a fast-growing tech company, he told me he had "jumped headfirst into AI." Within months, he was using it for nearly everything—staff updates, quarterly speeches, investor presentations. His method was simple: type bullet points into his favorite chatbot, add the words "make it inspiring," and then simply print the results on the pages he would refer to or the teleprompter he would read from.

At first, it felt like magic. His response time doubled when it came to answering emails and getting out reports. New investors who didn't really know him before he presented to them, complimented his polished clarity. He felt like he'd unlocked a secret edge.

But then came a quarterly town hall. He was now delivering before his team. He'd shared meals with some of them and traveled on off-sites with most of them. These were people who had known him for years. So, Ethan stood before them, looking sharp in a new suit for the occasion, and the words were elegantly flowing out of him. But something was off. The room wasn't engaged. Some team members seated in the first row looked up and smiled politely, but further back, you could see people looking at their phones and not at the stage.

"This doesn't sound like Ethan," one person said.

"It's like he's reading someone else's speech," another team member whispered.

They were both right.

Ethan's problem wasn't accuracy. His slides were polished. His sentences were elegant. But his speaking cadence was stiff. He wasn't fully aware of the meaning behind the words. His phrasing was clunky. Even his hand gestures felt pasted on. His eyes skimmed faces without *seeing* anyone. The spark that had once made him magnetic was gone. Without noticing and by no longer speaking from his heart, Ethan had not just outsourced his words, but also his *connecting presence*.

Presence is not a script. It's not a PowerPoint deck. It's the feeling people get when you're with them—that you are *here*, that you have *them* in mind, that the words are not simply true but *alive in your body*. Lose that, and people stop bringing you ideas. Over the next quarter, Ethan's team shifted to email. They assumed he'd rather scan bullet points than listen. His influence and ability to motivate people to action waned.

One of his direct reports finally got the courage to speak candidly with Ethan about what they were secretly calling his "disappearing act." That's when Ethan reached out to me for coaching. I didn't start by banning AI. Instead, I started by bringing him back into the room. We did walk-and-talks through the office, asking people what was on their mind. We rewrote his next address in *his* words. He practiced storytelling without any prompter, just memorizing a few key phrases, and introducing micro pauses so meanings could land and he could take time to look out into the room and actually *look* at his team members. We rehearsed a new technique: to ask the audience a question, *wait*, and then reflect back what he heard in real time before answering.

We didn't attempt drastic changes. We focused on amplifying real human interactions.

At the next town hall, he began with a story about a customer he'd visited the week before—describing the way the client's eyes lit up when a small fix saved a big headache. He connected the fix to the team behind it, he named names, he paused. You felt him *with* his people, not speaking *at* them. The applause was warmer. Afterward, three separate colleagues stopped him in the hallway to share ideas. Same role. Same slide template. Same man—but this time, Ethan had regained his *presence* by focusing on being *present*.

The Leader Who Leveled Up

Now meet "Sophie," a careful, scripted communicator. Competent, yes. Memorable, no. She once told me, "I'm just not a 'big presence' person." I smiled. Because:

***Presence isn't a personality type. It's a* skill *you can* develop.**

We met in her kitchen. Literally. I don't usually make house calls, but she happened to live near me, was a single mom with a pre-teen, and the only time to practice before her important quarterly update meeting was on a Tuesday night when her son would be at home and not at rugby practice. "So could you please come over for just an hour?"

As a fellow single mom, who understood the difficulty of getting babysitters at short notice, I agreed. When I arrived, he was sitting at the dining room table scrolling on his phone. "If I can get his attention," she joked, "I can capture anyone's."

Her first run-through was what you'd expect. Her eyes were fixed on her notes. Her tone was flat. I didn't work on changing her as much as we changed the *sequence*. She opened with a quick, human story of a conversation between herself and a colleague she would name check in the meeting.

Then she briefly paused before she revealed why the story was a scene setter for the quarterly report's main message. Headline. Support. Call to action. She tried again and we layered on more vocal energy. Then again. On the fifth run-through, her son, who had remained in the room the whole time, finally looked up. "Not bad," he said—which, from a pre-teen, is nearly the same as receiving a five-star review.

At the actual presentation, Sophie walked on without notes. She opened with the colleague's story she'd practiced, then invited the room to focus on the *main message*: "Here's what this tells us about how we're working—and what we can do next." It wasn't a performance; it was a conversation. Colleagues leaned in. "You were talking *to us*, not reading *at us*," one said afterward.

You may be asking yourself, "Where does the AI usage come in?" What I didn't explain was that Sophie had indeed used ChatGPT to help her brainstorm content and tighten structure. But she also asked me to help her rehearse and bring the content to life. On the day of the meeting, the voice was hers. AI made her create content *faster*. But she took the time to practice and refine and make herself *better*.

The Candidate Who Fell Flat

"Noah" was a recent college graduate with a brilliant mind and a problem. He used AI obsessively to prepare for interviews. Every possible question he could think of, he fed into a chatbot. He asked ChatGPT and Gemini and even Microsoft's Pilot to come up with new questions that he couldn't think of himself.

He memorized every answer with the exact polished phrasing that the AI assistant spat out for him.

The results were less than stellar. For instance, when an interview panel asked, "Tell us about a time you overcame a challenge," Noah recited a flawless paragraph. It sounded like perfection. But it just didn't sound like a real person. Afterward, during the debrief, the hiring manager told him: "You sounded like C-3PO. More android than human."

It's important to understand here that Noah didn't lose the job interview because of bad answers. He lost because he didn't connect. When we met a week later and he related all this to me, I asked him to *tell me* the same story as if we were two friends on a bus. He relaxed his shoulders and said, "Right—so there was this really hard deadline looming over me at the exact time that the prototype we were testing kept breaking..." and suddenly everything changed. His words weren't perfectly polished anymore, but his eyes, his hands, and his *energy* were all back in place. By using his own words and expressing himself freely, not merely reciting, Noah also freed up mental space for movement, eye contact, and energy that was previously consumed by memorization.

We rebuilt more personal answers for *all* of the questions. The next interview, he got an offer.

Polish without pulse feels plastic.

The CEO Who Resisted

Not all stories are cautionary. Some are happily contrarian. "Taz," a CEO I worked with in the Middle East, had a comms team who begged her to use AI for her speeches. She resisted. "I need to hear my own words," she said. "Otherwise, why would anyone believe me?"

We shaped her voice together. She practiced modulating tone, using silence as power, walking toward the person asking the hardest question. She learned to ask, "What am I missing?" and mean it. When she spoke, people didn't say, "What a great script." They said, "I trust her."

Ironically, by refusing an AI crutch, Taz made herself more future-proof. In a room full of synthetic sound, you could hear her human heart.

What AI Can't (and Won't) Do

AI can draft. AI can polish. AI can help you find an angle when you're stuck. Those are gifts. But AI cannot look someone in the eye. It cannot notice a furrowed brow and soften your tone. It cannot offer a smile that reassures, or choose integrity when deception would be easier. AI can't *earn* trust. Only you can.

Delegating your voice is not the same as *developing and amplifying* your voice. The latter is slower—yes. It's also the work that actually moves people.

Human Skills as Strategy

Across continents—from Saudi banks to Silicon Valley start-ups—I see the same pattern. As I've already mentioned, the leaders who thrive are not the ones with the slickest slide decks or the fastest prompts. They are the ones who ask a follow-up question because they care, who pause long enough for meaning to land, who really see the people gathered in the room rather than impersonally scanning like a sweeping spotlight, and who tell a story that makes others feel valued and uplifted.

Professor O'Boyle's point bears repeating:

The future won't be won by those who out-compute machines.
It will be won by those who out-connect them.

Two More Windows into Human Work

Let me add two brief stories to round out our chapter—places where AI's convenience almost cost the moment.

Alice led a regulated business and wrote a memo about a new, necessary policy. AI helped her produce a crisp document. The information was clear. But the reaction was ice.

"Another rule," people sighed. We rewrote the opening paragraph to start with the *human why*: the customer harm they were preventing, the employee stress they were reducing, the reputational risk they were avoiding. Same policy. New framing.

Next, and I really love this choice: we decided it would be impactful for her to record a two-minute selfie video for managers to play in team huddles. "Here's what this means for us. Here's how it helps. Here's what I'm asking from you—and what you can expect from me." Compliance went up. Complaints went down. Not because the policy changed, but because Alice's choices to make a more human *connection* did.

Omar was launching a division of his company in a new region. His slide deck was gorgeous—courtesy of AI and a design team. During rehearsal, I asked, "Where's the story?" He pointed to a slide full of logos. "No, Omar," I replied, "Where's *your* story. You are the presentation, not the slide deck. *You* must find a way to personally relate to all this."

He then told me about the first customer he'd ever lost, the mistake he'd made, the call he dreaded, and how he did it anyway. *That* story, which was vulnerable, real, and unvarnished, became his opener. He tied it to the region's stated mission: *"We do the brave thing; we make the hard call."* The deck was still there. But now his presentation included more human stories. Omar's human stories. I am confident his *message* and those *stories* lived in people long after they left the room.

From Autopilot to Intentional

If a machine can write your words, your responsibility to take more control of what words you are encouraging it to choose becomes greater. *What do you want to say? Why? To whom?* This is where my AIM methodology—**Audience, Intent, Message**—becomes your daily discipline.

Before you flip back to Chapter 7, here's a reminder:

- **Audience.** Who are they today? Not in the abstract. But as detailed as you can possibly imagine or know. What do they hope for? What do they fear? How tired are they? How proud? How skeptical?
- **Intent.** What do you want them to feel, think, and—most importantly of all—do by the end? If you can't say it in one sentence, you won't say it in twenty slides.
- **Message.** What single idea—said simply—would you want them to remember a week from now?

Of course, you can absolutely ask AI to brainstorm examples. But it can't read your mind. Only *you* can choose the audience you're serving, the intent you're aligning with, and the message that is true enough to be said simply and with inspiration.

Say It, Look It, Be It Again. In Practice

You've seen this throughout the book, but it's worth threading through the AI lens:

- **Say It.** Words that are initially crafted by AI can be tweaked to sound more like yours. You can start with a draft, but speak it aloud and listen. If it doesn't sound like the way you normally speak or use the vocabulary you would normally use, it won't land like you. Rewrite until your mouth and your message match.
- **Look It.** Your face and body can carry more connecting opportunities than your sentences. If your words are optimistic but your eyebrows knit in worry, people believe the brows. Try recording a one-minute rehearsal and watch it on mute. Does your face and your posture say what your paragraph says?
- **Be It.** This is the piece AI can't touch. The integrity that makes your message trustworthy. If you say "questions welcome," do you *really* welcome them? If you say "people first," does your calendar prove it? Are you pausing to ask questions or actively listen?

The Ten-Minute Voice Reclaim (A Gentle Practice)

No lists. No checkboxes. Just a small ritual you can try this week.

Pick one moment you're already going to have—a team huddle, a check-in, a client call. Before it starts, breathe and apply AIM. Who's here? What do I want for them to do? What's the one message I'm asking them to carry away?

Now, write a single *headline* sentence in plain language. Under it, one short story, stat, or example. Under that, one sentence that begins with, "So here's what this means for us..." That's it. Three lines. Then **say it out loud** once. Listen to your own voice. Tweak a word or two so it sounds like you. And go.

Do that once a week for a month. Watch what changes.

Meetings That Feel Like Humans Were There

Meetings are where culture lives or dies. AI can create the agenda. It cannot create the **moment**. Try a simple reframe: begin with a check-in question that points to what the meeting needs. "One word for how you're arriving."

"One highlight from the week." "One thing you're curious about today." Thirty seconds each. You'll shift the energy from *silent recipients* to *present participants*. End with a micro commitment: each person says one action they're taking as a result. Human bookends around the content. You'll feel the difference.

When You're Tired (Because You Will Be)

There will be days when you're tempted to let the machine speak for you. You're busy. You're travelling. You're juggling. On those days, give yourself grace—and still keep one human thing. Maybe it's a two-sentence personal opening. Maybe it's the extra thirty seconds to say a person's name and thank them for an unseen effort. Maybe it's one honest sentence: "I'm a little stretched today, but I'm glad to be here with you." People don't need perfect. They need **you**.

The Fear Beneath the Tool

A tool can't threaten you unless it's poking something vulnerable. For many, AI brushes against an old fear: *What if I'm not enough? What if I don't have anything special to say?* Let me say this plainly:

You are not being asked to* out-produce *a machine. You are being asked to* out-relate *it. Your value as a human is not in speed. It is in meaning.

The measure is not how quickly you can publish—it is how deeply you can connect.

So How Do You Human Up?

This isn't about rejecting AI. It's about reclaiming the parts of communication that will always be yours. Use AI in the early phases: idea-gathering, rough structure, draft language. Then do the final mile yourself. Read it out loud. If it doesn't sound like you, fix it. Practice with someone who will tell you the truth. Ask what they *felt*. Notice the nonverbals. Before the meeting, ask: *What state are these people in?* Meet them there. Remember: **be others-conscious to become less self-conscious.** The more you attend to the humans in front of you, the less you'll worry about yourself.

Your Real Advantage

Until the day a hologram can look someone in the eye with sincerity, your advantage is the warmth in your voice, the life in your eyes, and the integrity of your presence. Don't let speed cost you sincerity.

Don't trade connection for convenience.

Leadership isn't about how quickly you can push "publish." It's about how deeply you can connect. No algorithm, no chatbot, no polished paragraph will ever replace that. At least not yet.

Gina's Human-Up Notes

Keep AI in its lane—brainstorm and outline, yes. But for your final voice, no. Remember to always read your words aloud. Your mouth will tell you where they don't sound like you. Focus on the person across from you; it makes you less self-conscious and more real. Leave a little silence so meaning can land. Lead with empathy: *What might they be feeling right now?* Meet them there.

11 (Bonus!) Amplify You Case Studies

Amplified Applied

"You don't build a business; you build your people, and the people build the business."

—Zig Ziglar

People Just Like You Have Amplified Their Way to More Success

THE STORIES YOU ARE ABOUT TO READ ARE TRUE.

They are all real stories from real people I have been privileged to work with. The individual names have been changed, and their company identities intentionally obscured for obvious reasons, but the experiences, outcomes, and lessons are just as they occurred.

Some of these are success stories. One is a cautionary tale. But they all share elements in common: they are full of choices, decisions, and outcomes, which illustrate a range of *amplify* communication techniques and strategies.

The impact of our leadership—at work and beyond—arises from how we deliberately choose to *amplify* ourselves. Will we build the oars for our journey, fortify the legs of our communications stool, and shape the core of who we are? Will we choose to leave behind a legacy of human connected communications? This is something I try to do every day. I don't always get it right. But I try. Here's to hoping you are inspired to try too.

As you read these stories, I encourage you to think about how each person is—or isn't—effectively applying elements of the *amplify* approach.

Case Study #1 Veronica: The Campaign Concept

Working Visibly as a Leader—A Campaign for Continual Growth

Veronica, a regional leader for a global animal health organization, recently received her first 360-degree feedback report after stepping into her new role just three months ago.

With her results averaging well over four out of five in key areas like innovation, adaptability, urgency, motivation, calmness under pressure, and self-care, Veronica had clearly made a strong first impression. However, she knew that sustaining and building on this momentum required more than a good start. She needed a plan to translate this feedback into visible, actionable growth. This plan would show her team she was serious about not just hearing feedback but embedding it into her leadership practice.

The Campaign Concept

Veronica understood that sustaining her leadership effectiveness required intentionality and transparency. Instead of privately reflecting on her initial "first impression" results, I encouraged her to turn her growth journey into an active, visible and ongoing, team-centered campaign to signal to her team members and her managers that she was consistently demonstrating her awareness of how to *speak it!*, *look it!*, and *be it!*

This was not to be some kind of a corporate PR stunt, but a series of deliberate, authentic actions designed to engage her team, build trust, and model continuous improvement. So, she told everyone of her plan to essentially campaign her dedication to improvement. By inviting her colleagues into her development process, Veronica not only held herself accountable but also created space for open dialogue, mutual feedback, and shared progress. The campaign became a living example of the kind of culture she wanted to foster: one of humility, self-awareness, and growth.

I urged her to focus on three strengths from the 360-degree list that she wanted to actively continue showcasing and three areas for growth where she saw an opportunity to improve.

Veronica's three strengths she chose to highlight were: her ability to act as a catalyst for change, her calmness under pressure, and her skill in motivating others. These were areas where she had scored high in the feedback, and she wanted to ensure these qualities remained consistent. For her growth areas, Veronica chose to concentrate on providing clearer expectations to her team, increasing her accessibility, and reinforcing a balanced sense of urgency to encourage consistent, productive work. She knew that by openly sharing her goals and being accountable to her team, she could more effectively reinforce her commitment to continual improvement.

Making It Visible: The Open Commitment Campaign

Veronica began her campaign by openly sharing her feedback summary and focus areas with her team. She presented her plan during a team meeting, explaining that the feedback she'd received during her 360-degree review was essential in helping her serve them better and that she'd be focusing on key areas to ensure she consistently lived up to their expectations.

Using language that reinforced these goals, Veronica created a visible, ongoing commitment. For instance, when discussing timelines, she emphasized her focus on balancing urgency with clarity. When delegating tasks, she consciously checked in to confirm her expectations were clearly communicated. She regularly acknowledged the importance of accessibility, openly encouraging her team to reach out and engage actively in informal interactions. This open commitment approach made it clear to her team that Veronica was genuinely invested in maintaining her strong start while improving in areas that would help everyone work better together.

Regular Milestones and Mini Surveys

To sustain momentum, Veronica built checkpoints into her campaign. Rather than waiting another year for her next 360-degree review, she began conducting informal milestone surveys. Every few months, she invited her managers and team members to provide brief, anonymous feedback on her progress in her selected areas. By gathering regular insights, Veronica could fine-tune her approach, celebrate wins, and make adjustments before issues escalated.

This continuous feedback loop not only helped Veronica stay on track but also reinforced her commitment to her team. Her openness in seeking feedback fostered trust, showing her team that their perspectives were valued and that they played an active role in her development as a leader.

Results and Impact

Through this visible, actionable approach, Veronica's leadership style became a model of accountability and intentionality. She established a culture of feedback and growth, where team members could see their input reflected in her behavior and knew she was committed to mutual success. By the time her next formal review cycle rolled around, Veronica's team and peers were already aware of her efforts and could see tangible examples of her improvements.

Veronica's campaign illustrates how visible, intentional leadership creates a shared investment in growth. She didn't just work quietly behind the scenes to improve—she chose to model her development journey in real time. By applying her deeper understanding of how she communicates—through her voice, body language, and a growth-oriented mindset—Veronica began to signal, in every interaction, that she was there to support and elevate her team. Her mini campaign around performance goals became more than a strategy to sustain her strong start; it became a living, breathing commitment to consistency, clarity, and care.

She regularly referenced her development areas in team meetings, welcomed feedback as fuel, and adjusted her delivery to be more intentional—whether by pausing to invite input, softening her tone, or anchoring key messages with steady eye contact and grounded posture. In doing so, Veronica created a culture where growth was not only encouraged but expected—from herself first. This approach allowed her to continually evolve while bringing her team along with her—transforming feedback into progress, and progress into trust, alignment, and lasting impact.

Case Study #2 Paolo: Soften Your Face

Small Changes, Big Impact

At 62, Paolo is a seasoned leader managing a large countrywide organization. With over three decades in his field, he has cultivated a wealth of experience and a reputation for excellence. Known for his direct communication style and intense demeanor, Paolo has consistently achieved impressive results and earned the respect of his peers and team members. Recently, however, he discovered the profound impact that even small shifts in his behavior could have on those around him—especially his younger team members.

A Leader Who Cares Deeply About His Impact

Paolo received high scores across his recent 360-degree review, with strong positive feedback from both his managers and direct reports. These high scores validate his influence and affirm his commitment to inspiring those he leads. In line with his character, Paolo takes his impact on others seriously, understanding that his actions and approach can set the tone for his team's success. Recently, he hosted a large team-building retreat for 170 employees in Ibiza, Spain, a trip that strengthened his bond with the team and allowed them to celebrate their collective achievements.

Afterward, he was deeply moved by a video his team created to express their appreciation for him. The heartfelt video reflected the positive influence he has on those around him and served as a powerful reminder of his legacy. "It almost brought a tear to my eye," he admitted. Despite his considerable success and established reputation, this moment touched Paolo in a way that motivated him to continue honing his leadership.

Embracing His Influence

Paolo is beginning to recognize the significance of his presence, especially when entering a room. This is something he had heard before, but he hadn't fully appreciated until recently. His colleagues and team members have noted that his direct style, paired with an intense expression, can be intimidating, particularly for junior leaders. For them, Paolo's presence is often larger than life, and while this aura of authority serves him well in many instances, it can also create an unintended barrier. This insight opened Paolo's eyes to an aspect of his leadership that he could address with a small but meaningful adjustment.

The feedback Paolo received during his 360-degree review was simple: *situationally soften his facial expression and approach when interacting with junior team members.* By doing so, he would allow them to feel more comfortable, encouraging them to share openly. Paolo's reaction to this suggestion was immediate and affirmative. "I agree with it completely," he said. For him, this small change felt achievable and purposeful, and it aligned with his broader desire to make others feel valued and supported.

Why Small Adjustments Matter

For Paolo, who has naturally developed an intense style over the years, making subtle shifts in his approach might seem insignificant. But these minor adaptations can create a substantial difference in how junior colleagues perceive and work with him. By softening his expression, Paolo can signal openness and approachability, creating a safe space for others to voice their ideas and concerns. Such gestures, though small, can break down perceived hierarchies and foster trust, leading to stronger collaboration and more effective communication across the organization.

Paolo's story demonstrates that even leaders with extensive experience and a proven track record can make subtle adjustments to enhance their impact. These small changes didn't dilute his authority; instead, they reinforced his commitment to building meaningful connections. In his case, recognizing that his very presence has weight and power was crucial. He realized that, at times, a simple shift in tone or expression could set his team members at ease and make his influence even more constructive.

A Legacy of Compassionate Leadership

Paolo's dedication to his team has only intensified in recent years. Diagnosed with colon cancer a few years ago, he has gained a renewed perspective on the importance of each day. This experience reminds him that his work isn't just about achieving results but about building a legacy and nurturing those around him. Now, his focus extends beyond professional achievements to leave a lasting, positive influence on his team and ensure they feel supported and appreciated.

In our coaching sessions, I reflected this back to Paolo, emphasizing that his leadership journey continues to evolve. The legacy he has already built is formidable, but his openness to change signals his commitment to continuous growth. "You've already achieved so much," I reminded him, "and yet, your willingness to make these adjustments speaks volumes about the leader and person you are."

Small Actions, Big Results

As Paolo incorporates these small yet meaningful adjustments into his leadership style, he is reminded of the power of mindful communication. His readiness to implement a subtle shift in demeanor reflects his respect for his team members and his dedication to their development. By fostering an environment where his team feels at ease, Paolo not only strengthens individual relationships but also contributes to a culture of trust, openness, and growth.

Paolo's story exemplifies how even senior leaders with decades of experience can continue to evolve by focusing on the small things that make a big difference. His journey is a powerful reminder that leadership is a blend of authority and empathy and that sometimes, the smallest changes can have the most significant impact.

Paolo's commitment to his team and openness to adjust his approach is a reminder that, no matter how accomplished, leaders can always enhance their influence. As we consider his journey, we might ask ourselves: *What small changes can we make today to bring out the best in those around us?*

Case Study #3 William: Nailing the Boardroom Brief

A High-Stakes Board Presentation

William, a thirteen-year veteran with a global insurance firm in the United States, has built a strong career in risk management. Known for his meticulous attention to detail, he's highly regarded for his expertise in analyzing data and evaluating risk. However, when his vice president selected him to lead the company's annual group presentation before the board, William faced a new challenge. This role would require him to elevate his language, project confidence, and facilitate seamlessly among five other department heads who would also be presenting.

Even though William had a strong reputation inside the company, he knew this high-profile presentation called for something extra—more adaptability, more presence. In our coaching sessions, we worked on helping him strike the right balance between his natural eye for detail and the bigger-picture thinking that senior executives want to hear about. It was a case of shifting gears so he could connect at a more strategic level.

Understanding the Opportunity and Identifying Key Goals

As we began our coaching journey, I wanted to understand William's mindset and explore his vision for this presentation. Together, we broke down the expectations his leadership team had of him in this role. He expressed his concern about staying clear, concise, and captivating—skills he felt he had yet to fully develop. Additionally, he was tasked with not only presenting his own segment but also moderating an interactive discussion among other department heads, a responsibility that added a layer of complexity to his role.

Together, we set three key goals for William:

1. **Elevating His Language.** Moving from detail-heavy descriptions to concise, high-impact statements.
2. **Projecting Confidence.** Using body language, tone, and delivery techniques to reinforce his presence as the presentation's lead.
3. **Effective Facilitation.** Developing skills to manage transitions fluidly, involve other presenters, and maintain engagement throughout.

Strengthening Communication Techniques

A critical part of our work together involved helping William move away from the granular details he naturally gravitated toward. I encouraged him to focus on the big-picture themes that would resonate with the board: risk trends, high-level solutions, and key strategic opportunities.

To refine his language, we worked on two communication techniques:

- **The Three-Point Rule.** I encouraged him to summarize each of his talking points in a structure of not more than three key insights. This method keeps information digestible and would ensure that the board retained critical takeaways.
- **Shifting from Data to Storytelling.** We worked on turning complex data into clear, compelling stories. Instead of just rattling off numbers, William learned to frame them in a way that made the message stick. For instance, rather than listing percentages in risk categories, he opened with a scenario: "Imagine the impact on our portfolio if these risk factors tick up by even one percent."That simple shift helped his audience see not just the data but the potential consequences. It wasn't about dumbing things down, it was about making the numbers matter.
- **Body Language and Building Confidence.** William's challenge with projecting confidence became evident when we discussed his approach to body language and eye contact. His natural inclination was to look down at his notes frequently, which he felt helped him stay grounded but inadvertently projected a lack of confidence.

We focused on two physical techniques to help him project authority and connect with the board:

- **The Power Stance.** A grounded, shoulders-back stance that opens up the body and conveys presence and approachability. We practiced this stance in our sessions until it felt natural for him.
- **Intentional Eye Contact.** I encouraged William to hold the room by slowly sweeping his gaze across the audience. This practice would keep his focus outward and help him maintain engagement, while also reducing any inclination to rely on his notes.

These techniques, though seemingly simple, made all the difference. William began to see how a few intentional adjustments could *amplify* his confidence and poise.

Leading the Team with Composure

Finally, we turned to facilitation techniques to help him seamlessly transition between speakers. For the discussion section, where each department head would speak to their area of expertise, William's task was to set a collaborative tone while maintaining the presentation's flow.

Together, we created a script for bridging phrases that allowed him to acknowledge each presenter and link their points back to the central theme. These sounded like, "Thank you, Sarah, for that insight on financial controls. Next, we'll hear from James, who will discuss emerging risk trends and how they intersect with our financial strategies." This approach allowed William to keep the presentation cohesive and made each speaker feel acknowledged and involved.

Stepping into the Role with Confidence

As William practiced these skills, he began to feel more comfortable in his role as the presentation leader. The combination of using elevated language, strong body language, and effective facilitation gave him the ability to handle unexpected moments. When the day arrived, William delivered a polished and strategic presentation that resonated with the board and earned positive feedback from both his team and executives.

William's case highlights that, even for seasoned professionals, refining communication and leadership skills can have an enormous impact. With each small adjustment, William became a more confident and capable presenter, embodying the kind of composure and clarity that resonated with his high-level audience. For leaders like William, these subtle, incremental changes can indeed lead to significant professional growth.

Case Study #4 Michael: No Time Outs

Hitting the Ground Running

When Michael stepped into his new role as vice president overseeing a major region in his healthcare company—including countries like Japan, China, the Philippines, and Singapore—he knew there was no time to ease in. The scope was big, the teams were diverse, and the expectations were high. From the start, he made it a priority to connect with the people behind the operations—not just the processes. That's why he kicked things off with an in-person tour, visiting manufacturing plants across the region to listen, learn, and build relationships.

Each stop brought its own set of demands. During one of our coaching sessions, he said: "this tour was a marathon. I'd land, jump into meetings, tour the plant, and then take another red-eye flight to the next country. Sleep was rare, and I was running on fumes." Even through exhaustion, his determination remained steady. "I realized there are no timeouts in leadership. These are my people—they deserve my full presence and attention."

Michael recalled one especially tiring evening. After arriving late at night, he was set to meet the senior leadership team for breakfast the next morning. This gathering was his opportunity to connect with local leaders and share his vision.

"That night," he admitted, "I could've easily canceled or postponed, but that wasn't an option. I had to show up for them, just like I'd want any leader to show up for me."

Bringing Resolve to Leadership

Despite his fatigue, Michael committed to giving his all. "I walked into that breakfast with my eyes wide open, my voice enthusiastic, and my focus dialed in," he said. "Because that's what those leaders needed. They needed to feel like they had all of me, not just a part of me."

He knew that showing up less than fully engaged would signal a lack of respect and priority. "It wouldn't have been fair if I showed up bright and engaged for one country's team, then half-hearted for another. That's the last impression I wanted to leave."

His words during our session underscored his belief: "Sometimes, when you don't feel like it, you show up anyway," he said. "And you don't just show up—you bring your best, even if it means summoning every ounce of resolve you have left."

As we explored this idea in coaching, I encouraged Michael to view this approach as situational awareness—a leader's commitment to amplifying themselves requires them to understand the needs of each moment. "It doesn't mean pushing yourself to burnout," I noted, "but recognizing what's required and delivering on that."

"Exactly, Gina," he agreed. "It's not about pretending you're invincible. It's about knowing when you're needed and stepping up."

Balancing Presence and Renewal

Through our conversations, Michael began to see leadership as a balance between exertion and renewal. He realized that his every action—whether intentional or not—sent a message to his teams. With that understanding, he committed to building moments of recovery into his routine, and recognizing that his teams deserved not just a present leader but a sustainable one.

By fully engaging with each team, despite his personal fatigue, Michael laid the foundation for trust, respect, and open communication. His actions set a high standard for leadership—not merely as a title but as a day-to-day commitment to serve, connect, and inspire.

Michael's mantra, "There are no timeouts in leadership," reminds us all of the power of presence. When leaders bring their full selves to the room, they create a lasting impact—one that can be seen, felt, and trusted.

Case Study #5 Sharifa: Consider the Pictures in the Other Person's Head First

When Pressure Builds at the Top

Sharifa is the chief HR officer for a major hospitality development project—and with the company expanding fast, her world has become a whirlwind of new hires, shifting workflows, and constant change. In one of our recent coaching sessions, she opened up about just how intense it's been. The pace and pressure were starting to affect her health, and she felt overwhelmed and frustrated. On top of that, she noticed a growing distance between herself and the CEO, who was under his own mountain of stress—juggling senior leaders and racing to secure key funding. It was a tough space for both of them, and it called for a fresh way to reconnect and realign.

"I'm just so frustrated," Sharifa admitted. She was considering using their upcoming meeting as an opportunity to unload her concerns. However, we discussed an alternate approach. I suggested that rather than leading with her frustrations, she could apply AIM. Remember, that's the call to consider your audience first. Before you try to move to your own goals and intent. And long before you deliver your message points. Think about the CEO. What might he be going through? "Ask how he's doing first," I advised. "Let him know you recognize the weight he's carrying, that you understand how lonely it can be at the top, and that you're there to support him."

A Transformative Conversation

Shortly after her meeting, Sharifa called back, energized and deeply moved. "Gina, it was the best meeting we've ever had," she shared. Sharifa explained how she opened by acknowledging his pressure, expressing empathy, and offering her support. This small shift in approach changed the entire dynamic. Her CEO visibly relaxed, even appearing emotional. He said he hadn't felt like himself lately and admitted to feeling overwhelmed. He expressed genuine gratitude for her understanding and support, confiding that he wanted to refocus on being a proactive, compassionate leader.

The conversation allowed both Sharifa and her CEO to reconnect on a more personal level. Where Sharifa had once felt a transactional distance between them, this meeting re-established a peer-to-peer relationship built on mutual respect and shared pressures.

Building Connection through AIM and Empathy

For Sharifa, this experience was transformative. By setting aside her own frustrations to show empathy first, she created an open, safe space that allowed her CEO to share honestly. This approach not only renewed her connection with him but also reinforced her role as a supportive and trusted leader.

My takeaway from this experience is a reminder: sometimes, to receive care, we must first extend it to others. By reaching out with empathy, Sharifa restored a sense of teamwork and support within her leadership relationship, showing that sometimes the most effective way to ease our own challenges is to begin by lightening the load of those around us.

Case Study #6 Liam: Cracks at the Top

When the CEO Undermines the Culture

Liam was the CEO of a global company with thousands of employees. Charismatic but impulsive, he prided himself on being provocative online. That backfired spectacularly when a series of his tweets—derogatory, inflammatory, and completely unrelated to the business—went viral. The backlash forced him to temporarily step down.

A new CEO was appointed, but after only a few months, they abruptly left. It created a state of whiplash across the company. Employees were tired. Jaded. And deeply unsure of who or what to trust. When Liam resumed his role, the company's leadership and learning and development (L&D) teams reached out to me. They knew something had to change—and fast.

The brief? Help them rebuild trust. Recenter the culture around compassionate communication. And hopefully remind everyone that leadership isn't just about power. It's about presence.

When Leaders Check Out, Employees Tune Out

When I launched the first virtual training session, I could feel the tension through the screen. While some team members were warm and engaged, a vocal few pushed back hard. "This is too basic," someone scoffed. Another chimed in, "We already know this stuff."

But here's the thing: they didn't. Not really.

Because communication is never just about knowing. It's about showing.

And unfortunately, their leader wasn't showing up. Liam had declined to attend the session entirely. He even unsubscribed from my support email series after the very first update. That single act—small on the surface—spoke volumes. The person with the most influence had effectively said, "This doesn't matter to me." And when the leader checks out, the rest of the team inevitably wonders why they should bother checking in.

Culture Change Is a Contact Sport

To rebuild a culture, especially after a scandal, you need consistency and care. You need leaders who are willing to walk the walk, not just delegate the tough stuff to HR or comms and hope the dust settles. That's not how trust works.

The leadership development sessions continued, and while we made progress with some pockets of the organization, others remained disengaged. The L&D director asked for my honest take. And I gave it: the root of the resistance wasn't the content. It was Liam's lack of visible commitment. Without him modeling empathy, curiosity, and accountability, those concepts felt optional—even performative—to everyone else.

Case Study #7 Julia: Practice Out Loud

Elevating Presentation Impact through Rehearsal

Julia, the global sales director for a leading engineering company, is no stranger to high-stakes presentations. Her role requires her to represent the company worldwide, discussing its capabilities, growth projections, and strategic direction with diverse audiences, including senior clients and board members.

While Julia had a thorough understanding of her material, she has historically struggled to deliver it with the smoothness and clarity she desired. Her presentations tended to feel disjointed, marked by frequent filler words like "uh" and "you know," which disrupted her flow and lessened the impact of her insights. Sometimes she found herself trailing off without a clear, memorable closing statement, leaving her audience with no strong takeaway.

In our first coaching session, we identified that the root of this issue was a lack of out-loud rehearsal. Although she reviewed her materials countless times, Julia admitted she never practiced delivering them audibly. We decided to focus on this approach as she prepared for an important quarterly meeting, a setting where clarity, confidence, and authority were essential. By dedicating over an hour to practicing aloud, Julia aimed to not only refine her phrasing and transitions but also lock in key messages, ensuring she would leave her audience with a powerful closing message.

Out Loud Outcome Outstanding

For her practice, Julia didn't simply run through her entire presentation in one sitting. Instead, she broke it into segments, focusing on what we called the "power phrases"—those carefully crafted lines intended to resonate with the attendees long after the meeting concluded. She worked on perfecting her opening, then honed her transitions, and finally put special emphasis on the closing, envisioning it as a moment to deliver a clear, memorable takeaway. By focusing on one section at a time, Julia was able to internalize each part of her message without becoming overwhelmed.

After the meeting, Julia experienced a profound shift in both her delivery and her confidence. Her once-frequent filler words were significantly reduced, allowing her insights to come through with greater clarity and impact. She felt a smoother rhythm in her presentation, which helped her speak with newfound confidence. Most importantly, she was able to conclude her remarks with a strong, high-level takeaway, leaving the board members with a clear sense of direction. Reflecting on the experience, Julia noted, "It's the little things—like rehearsing my phrases out loud—that have a significant impact not only on how I deliver but on how I feel about my delivery."

The feedback from her audience echoed this improvement. Her supervisor commented on the clarity and confidence of her presentation and mentioned how well she landed her key points. This affirmation reinforced for Julia the value of intentional, vocalized practice and how it elevated her communication.

Julia's journey underscores a valuable lesson: powerful presentations don't just happen—they're built through focused, intentional practice. By putting in the time to rehearse out loud, Julia transformed her delivery and strengthened her connection with her audience, and she's already seeing how these refinements can have a lasting positive impact on her professional presence.

Case Study #8 Alexander: The Social Butterfly

Is "Winging It" Really That Wise?

Alexander, a senior manager at a top tech company in Singapore, is as outgoing as they come. "I'm a social butterfly," he said with a grin during one of my presentation skills workshops. He thrives on interaction, loves being around people, and takes pride in his off-the-cuff style. Spontaneity, for him, was his calling card.

As I discussed the importance of rehearsal in presentations with him and about twenty other senior managers, Alexander interjected, "Oh, I never rehearse—it ruins the spontaneity." Laughter rippled through the room, and one of his colleagues seized the moment to reply, "That's why we never know what you're trying to say. You wander all over the place, and we miss the point."

There was even more laughter. Alexander's face registered a mix of surprise and embarrassment. It was clear that while he was well liked, his reluctance to prepare was affecting how his colleagues perceived his communication effectiveness.

Creating Some Rehearsal Guardrails to Keep on Track

Alexander's natural charisma and quick wit were strengths, but his presentations lacked focus and clarity. His aversion to rehearsal stemmed from a fear of appearing overly rehearsed or losing his ability to connect with his audience in the moment. Yet his wing-it approach was leading to frustration among his colleagues, who struggled to follow his often meandering delivery.

Rather than dismissing Alexander's concern about spontaneity, I reframed the concept of rehearsal for him. "Rehearsing doesn't mean memorizing every word," I explained. "It's about getting comfortable with your material so that you can be both confident and flexible." I suggested he start with these steps:

1. **Outline Key Messages.** We worked together to identify the central ideas he wanted to convey. Instead of scripting every word, we focused on a clear structure: an engaging opening, three key points, and a memorable close.
2. **Practice with Purpose.** To address his concern about spontaneity, I encouraged him to rehearse aloud—not to completely memorize everything, just a few power phrases, his main headline, and closing takeaway. Speaking aloud helped him to refine his phrasing and timing. I also recommended recording himself and watching the playback to assess his delivery.
3. **Feedback Loop.** We set up a practice session with another colleague. This allowed Alexander to simulate presenting in a

low-stakes environment while receiving constructive feedback on areas like clarity and pacing.

In his next team presentation, the difference was clear, and so was Alexander. He opened with a concise statement of purpose, followed by well-structured points that kept his audience engaged. His natural humor and energy still shone through, but this time, it was anchored by a sense of direction.

After the presentation, the colleague who had previously criticized his approach gave him a thumbs-up and said, "That was spot on, Alex. I actually knew what you were saying this time!"

Alexander later admitted, "I was skeptical, but rehearsing didn't kill my spontaneity. It actually gave me more confidence to be myself because I wasn't scrambling to think of what to say next."

Alexander's story highlights a critical lesson: even the most naturally charismatic communicators benefit from preparation. Rehearsal isn't about stifling spontaneity; it's about creating a framework that allows your personality and message to shine.

Case Study #9 Kenji: Pump Up the Volume

Building Confidence, One Phrase at a Time

When I started working with Kenji, a regional communications leader in a global healthcare company, his challenge wasn't content—it was *delivery*. He was thoughtful, clear, and highly respected behind the scenes. But in meetings, especially with senior leaders, his soft-spoken style made him easy to overlook. People often asked him to repeat himself, not because he didn't know what he was talking about—but because his voice simply didn't carry the authority he already had.

So, in our sessions, we didn't just talk about *what* he needed to say—we focused on *how* he needed to say it.

We began with a deceptively simple warm-up: saying "Good morning, everyone" out loud, again and again, until it sounded intentional, strong, and purposeful. We treated it like a vocal "power stance"—a phrase that, with the right volume, tone, and pacing, could set the tone for the entire meeting. And guess what? Just practicing that one line a few times helped Kenji feel more grounded from the very first word.

Then we tackled what I like to call "runway phrases"—short, go-to lines that keep your authority while buying you time to think. These phrases give your thoughts space to take off with clarity and calm. For example:

- "Here's the key point I'd like to emphasize…"
- "I hear what you're saying, and let me also add…"
- "To build on that thought…"

These weren't robotic scripts. They were intentional tools—simple, reliable phrases that Kenji could pull out anytime he needed to project confidence, step into a conversation, or gather his thoughts under pressure. Saying them out loud, repeatedly, helped him build what I have already shared with you—the power of building "muscle memory for your message." The more he practiced, the more natural it became to speak up with clarity and presence—even in high-stakes situations.

Say It! Look It! Be It!

I reminded Kenji that communication is never just about the words. It's the full package:

- **Say it**—with confident tone and pacing.
- **Look it**—through calm posture and eye contact.
- **Be it**—by showing conviction through facial expression and presence.

When those three elements work together, your message carries weight—and so do you.

Kenji began to see how this wasn't about overthinking or overperforming. It was about aligning how he *felt* with how he *showed up*. Instead of second-guessing himself or apologizing with his volume, he started owning his space. The same way he helped others tell the story of a medical breakthrough, he was now learning to tell *his* story—starting with his voice.

Call-Out: "Isn't This All a Bit Much?"

I know what some of you might be thinking: "Do I really need to rehearse how to say 'Good morning' or prep a few lines before every meeting? Isn't that a bit… extra?"

Here's my honest answer: not at all.

In fact, I think not practicing is what holds so many brilliant professionals back.

Sure, you can "wing it" for years and hope it all clicks. Or you can choose to be intentional. You can say, look, and be the communicator your role requires. That's not fake. It's focused. And it works.

Communication Is a Skill. And Skills Are Built

Kenji quickly got on board with this idea. What felt a little awkward at first—deliberately repeating phrases out loud, adjusting his tone, practicing openers—soon began to feel empowering. Just like any technical skill, this kind of repetition leads to fluency. It doesn't make you robotic. It makes you ready.

We even had a little fun with it. I encouraged him to think of these tools like Lego bricks—small, versatile pieces that, when combined, could build something strong, flexible, and uniquely his. A confident opener here. A clarifying follow-up there. A grounding phrase when things got tense. With each new brick, Kenji gained a little more control over how he came across—and how much impact his words had.

Our session laid the foundation for a new kind of communication style—one that was less about being spontaneous and more about being *deliberate*. Because that's what leadership communication really is: not a talent, but a choice. A series of consistent behaviors that, over time, amplify your voice and your influence.

Kenji walked away with more than a few helpful phrases. He left with a personal communication toolkit—and the understanding that presence isn't something you're born with. It's something you build. One brick at a time.

Case Study #10 Beatrice: Holding Her Ground

Stop Second-Guessing and Show Up as the Leader You Are

Beatrice had the title. She had the expertise. What she didn't yet have was the *confidence*. As a newly hired plant manager for a major pharmaceutical company in Johannesburg—brought on during Covid lockdowns—she'd spent her first year interacting only through screens. No hallway chats. No shared coffee breaks. And no real opportunity to build rapport with her peers, all of whom were male and running plants across the region. The unspoken hierarchy in virtual meetings was clear—and Beatrice often found herself hesitating to jump in, holding back, or getting talked over entirely. She didn't need more qualifications. She needed a mindset shift—and a few practical tools—to start owning her space in the (virtual) room.

During our coaching sessions, Beatrice confessed she struggled to contribute effectively in these remote regional meetings. Despite practicing strong opening "runway" lines I gave her (much like I gave to Kenji above), such as "I would like to add a point here," and working on maintaining her volume and smooth delivery, her confidence still wavered. For three weeks, after each meeting, she would return to our sessions, saying, "It didn't go great."

It turned out her discomfort ran deeper than the remote setting. Over time, Beatrice revealed that her father had been extremely strict when she was a child, forbidding her and her sister to speak unless spoken to first. This upbringing had left a lasting impact on her confidence, particularly in male-dominated environments.

Recognizing the complexity of her situation, I suggested a multi-pronged approach. First, we continued role-playing scenarios to build her communication skills. I also encouraged her to schedule one-on-one remote calls with her peers to foster personal connections beyond the formal meeting setting. Finally, I recommended she seek professional counseling to address the deeper psychological barriers rooted in her past.

Within just a few months, Beatrice wasn't just participating in meetings—she was leading them. The blend of practical strategies, mindset shifts, and real human support gave her the tools—and the self-belief—she needed to step fully into her role. And when the company finally held its first in-person leadership retreat, Beatrice didn't just show up. She *owned* the room. Confident, connected, and clearly respected by her peers, she stood out not just as a capable manager, but as a true leader.

Her journey is a powerful reminder that it's not just about knowing what to say—it's about believing you deserve to say it. And when you do, everything changes.

Case Study #11 Freya: Dressing the Part, Owning the Role

How a Style Reboot Can Help You Step Back into Leadership with Clarity and Confidence

When Freya returned to work after nearly ten years raising her two children, she brought her sharp mind and deep expertise as a chemical engineer—but she left something behind: confidence in how she showed up.

Stepping into a more senior role, she quickly realized that her old wardrobe—and even her overall presence—no longer matched the leader she was becoming. Her supervisor saw it too and wisely suggested some support. That's when I stepped in to help Freya not just update her look, but refresh the way she saw—and carried—herself in this next chapter of her career.

Freya's clothing wasn't just outdated—it no longer fit her in a flattering or professional way. Her style reflected that of a more junior employee, which clashed with the senior responsibilities her new role demanded. She would be representing her company in meetings with senior executives and government officials, and her appearance needed to reflect the authority and credibility she brought to the table.

In our initial meeting, I sought to understand Freya's personal style, preferences, and the practicalities of her busy life as a mother of two school-aged children. With this in mind, I created a tailored PowerPoint lookbook to guide her transformation.

The lookbook featured ensembles that prioritized efficiency and elegance—ideal for a professional and a mom juggling multiple demands. Neutral colors, simple cuts, and versatile pieces were central to the recommendations. These allowed for easy mix-and-match combinations, saving her time while ensuring she always appeared polished. We included shoes with structured, low heels that combined comfort with presence, along with accessories that subtly elevated her look.

Freya embraced these changes with enthusiasm. Within weeks, she began receiving positive feedback from colleagues and felt her confidence soar. She transitioned seamlessly into her new role, commanding respect in every meeting she attended. This case highlights how thoughtful, intentional updates to one's professional wardrobe can significantly boost confidence and credibility, enabling leaders just like you to shine in high-stakes environments.

"If you think something is too small to make a difference, you haven't spent the night with a mosquito."

—African Proverb

Acknowledgments

To my clients over the years: you have been my greatest teachers and my constant reminders that this work matters. You've shown me that communicating with purpose and intention takes effort—but that the payoff is profound. Every time someone tells me, "Oh, I get it! I can do this!" it fills me with happiness and confirms that these skills are transferable and life-changing. Each of us has a light within us, capable of illuminating the paths of others. In a world that can be both challenging and isolating, proactive communication and genuine connection are essential.

As Dr. Bob Waldinger, Harvard University's director of the world's longest study on happiness, told me, "Most of us will feel happier when we make active connections."

And as executive coach and entrepreneur, Rhett Power, said to me from the World Economic Forum in Davos, Switzerland, "AI cannot replace the soft skills leaders need: presenting, networking, and team building. These are the skills that inspire trust and loyalty."

Their words reinforce the importance of what I have the privilege to teach.

To my amazing daughter, Lulu: you are the greatest joy—and challenge—of my life. To my brother Brad and sister Andrea, who share in my story and whose love has anchored me through the years, and of course to my indomitable, role-model mother who is my hero and personifies discipline, determination, and persistence.

To my first mentor in the news business, WTTG Fox 5 anchor Ron Gardner, and my business mentor here in Ireland, Paul Connolly, thank you for shaping my path with your wisdom, guidance, and special brands of humor.

To my incredible Language of Leadership, Ltd. team: David, Samantha, Roz, Anita, Pierce, Eoin, and my two invaluable assistants, Dorota (at the beginning) and now Julia—you all have kept me grounded and make everything I do possible.

Finally, to two bestselling leadership authors who have also influenced this journey: Liz Wiseman, for challenging me to refine the "big idea" of this book and for reminding me that bringing our best selves to work is an aspiration worth pursuing in a world that often calls for us to simply "be ourselves" and Dave Jennings, for the best advice anyone could give an aspiring author: *"The worst book you publish is better than the best book you never finish."*

To everyone who has played a part, my gratitude is endless. Thank you for your inspiration, support, and belief in the power of positive and proactive leadership communications, that anyone can apply to amplify their impact.

About the Author

Gina London is an Emmy-winning former journalist, ICF-certified executive coach, and founder of Language of Leadership, Ltd. A former CNN anchor and correspondent, she spent more than a decade reporting on global business, politics, and culture before advising senior leaders and organizations across more than fifty countries. Gina works with Fortune 500 companies, government agencies, and leadership teams to strengthen executive presence, clarity, and human connection. Based in Ireland, she writes a weekly leadership and communication column for *The Sunday Independent.*

Epilogue: A Celebration of Connection

Back in Chapter 1, I shared the story of meeting Archbishop Desmond Tutu for the first time as a young reporter in Orlando. His joyful presence and unwavering commitment to lifting others stayed with me for years.

Nearly two decades later, in 2018, our paths crossed again—this time in Cape Town, where I had the incredible honor of serving as Master of Ceremonies for the International Children's Peace Prize. Archbishop Tutu, the patron of the KidsRights Foundation that hosted the event, joined us on stage to present the awards. His spirit—though physically more fragile—was as vibrant and infectious as ever.

As the ceremony concluded, the Soweto Gospel Choir gathered on stage, the children stood proudly with their prizes, and I was filled with that quiet satisfaction of a job well done. Then something extraordinary happened.

Archbishop Tutu, who had remained seated for most of the event, slowly rose from his wheelchair. The room fell silent. With a gentle but firm voice, he pointed toward me and said, "We need to take a moment and celebrate *her*." He continued, "Gina has brought a delightful energy and enthusiasm to today that we are all better for."

He took my hand—and to my astonishment—began slowly to dance with me. The choir picked up his cue, music filled the room, and together we moved in joy, surrounded by applause. It was a spontaneous moment of connection, generosity, and grace. And it was also the last time I would share space with him.

But that moment became a lasting lesson. Because Archbishop Tutu didn't just recognize me—he modeled something timeless. He showed, once again, that true leadership means using your platform to lift others. That joy and strength, compassion and authority, can and *should* coexist.

So, in his spirit, I want to celebrate *you.*

For choosing to read this book.
For committing to your growth.
For stepping into the kind of leadership that uplifts, includes, and connects.

You've taken meaningful steps to amplify your voice, your presence, and your purpose. And as you carry that forward into your work and life, I hope you'll remember: **the most powerful leaders aren't the ones who take the spotlight—but the ones who know how to share it**.

Here's to all you're becoming.

With every kindness
—Gina

Fifteen Power Phrases to Further Amplify You

Fresh Language to Help You Connect, Encourage, and Lead with More Clarity and Care

YOU'VE MADE IT THROUGH *Amplify You*.

I hope you're feeling more confident, intentional, and inspired in how you connect with others. But before we close, here's one final set of tools to take with you.

I'm often asked by leaders, *"Can you just give me a few go-to phrases I can use in the moment—especially when I'm stuck or feeling flat?"* Absolutely. Even the most experienced communicators can fall into autopilot. We rely on the same familiar phrases without realizing we're missing opportunities to be more encouraging, curious, or clear.

So, here's a collection of fifteen of my "runway" phrases—conversation starters, relationship builders, and leadership softeners or strengtheners—that you can add to your daily lexicon. These are designed to help you stretch your vocabulary, shift your tone, and spark better conversations.

Try a few out in your next meeting. See what lands. And, as always, let me know what works for you.

1. **"What's one thing you've always wanted to try with this project? Let's explore it together."**
   Use this to spark creativity and empower team members to take risks.
   Encourage bold thinking by inviting team members to pitch fresh ideas they may have been hesitant to share. Follow up by collaboratively evaluating its feasibility.
2. **"Can you walk me through your perspective? I'd love to see this through your eyes."**
   Demonstrates a genuine willingness to understand and appreciate unique viewpoints.
   This builds trust, especially in moments of tension or differing opinions. It shows that you really do value their input.
3. **"Let's kick this off by sharing something that's been inspiring us this week—work-related or not."**
   An icebreaker that humanizes team meetings. Think of creating a connection before diving into content.
   It sets a positive tone and encourages team members to share a bit of their personal world, building camaraderie.
4. **"If you had all the resources in the world, how would you tackle this?"**
   Gives autonomy and encourages strategic thinking.
   This question removes immediate constraints and helps the team visualize optimal solutions, which can often lead to practical, scaled-down versions.
5. **"I'm not 100% sure about the best path here—what's your take?"**
   Demonstrates vulnerability and invites collaboration.
   Transparency about not having all the answers shows humility, inspiring others to contribute and share ownership of decisions.
6. **"What would it look like if we tackled this in a completely opposite way?"**
   Promotes innovative and disruptive problem-solving.
   Challenge traditional thinking by flipping the usual approach, encouraging creative, out-of-the-box ideas.

7. **"This is your call to make. I trust you to own it. Let me know how I can support you."**
   Provides autonomy and reinforces trust.
   Leaders empower their team by clearly communicating confidence in their abilities while standing by for guidance if needed.

8. **"Let's hit pause on tactics for a second. What's our ultimate goal here, and how does this help us get there?"**
   Centers the team on strategic alignment.
   A perfect phrase for redirecting when the team gets bogged down in details, bringing focus back to the bigger picture.

9. **"If we could change one thing about how we work together, what would it be?"**
   Encourages open feedback and continuous improvement.
   This question fosters dialogue about team dynamics in a constructive way and empowers the group to cocreate solutions.

10. **"Let's celebrate a small win today—what's one thing you're proud of from this week?"**
    Keeps morale high by recognizing incremental progress. Creates another "connection before content" opportunity.
    This encourages reflection on individual contributions and creates a culture of consistent acknowledgment.

11. **"Before we leave today, let's each share one question we still have. There's no such thing as a bad question."**
    Turns uncertainty into a strength by making it normal to ask questions.
    This tactic builds a culture of curiosity and continuous learning.

12. **"Can you take the lead on this? I think your approach would really make an impact here."**
    Empowers team members by recognizing their unique strengths.
    This phrase fosters confidence and ownership by explicitly tying the opportunity to their expertise.

13. **"Here is where I think I fell short recently. What's one thing you think I could have done better?"**
    Demonstrates transparency and invites feedback.
    By modeling self-awareness and openness to growth, leaders set the tone for the entire team to improve.

14. **"Let's each share one word to describe how we're feeling before we dive in."**

    A quick check-in tool to set the emotional tone for a meeting. Remember "connection before content."

    It makes room for emotions, letting the team feel seen and setting a supportive atmosphere.

15. **"What's the one thing you need from me to feel more confident moving forward?"**

    Provides focused, actionable support.

    By asking directly, you are asking your team members to specify their needs and avoid overloading them with unnecessary input or jumping to your own conclusions.

Speaking of Endings... but Really, New Beginnings

As we wrap up this journey together, I hope these pages have sparked a few "aha" moments for you—maybe even answered something you didn't realize you were wondering about.

By now, you've seen how each chapter of *Amplify You* builds on the last—like stepping stones guiding you toward becoming a more intentional, impactful version of yourself. Whether it was learning to command a room, connect more authentically, or communicate with greater clarity, my goal has always been to give you practical, human tools you can actually *use*—at work, and in life.

Take a moment to think back to the beginning of the book. Do you remember that number-line exercise on page 23? I asked you to choose a number that reflected how confident you felt in your leadership communication and connection skills.

Now, look at that number again.

Even if you've nudged it just one number higher—even if you've started testing a new technique or shifting an old mindset—*that's progress.* Real, measurable, meaningful progress.

And it's only the beginning.

So, as you close this final section, don't just shut the book. Take a breath. Picture the version of you who shows up with clarity, care, and confidence. Keep building that version, one step, one choice, one conversation at a time.

You're not just reading *Amplify You.* You're living it.

And I'm cheering you on every step of the way.

Amplifying the way you communicate and connect is about progression, not perfection.

Notes

Chapter 2

1. Amy J. C. Cuddy, Susan T. Fiske, and Peter Glick, "Warmth and Competence as Universal Dimensions of Social Perception: The Stereotype Content Model and the BIAS Map," *Advances in Experimental Social Psychology* 40 (2008): 61–149. Accessed January 28, 2025. https://www.sciencedirect.com/science/article/pii/S0065260108600020.
2. Stuart Diamond, *Getting More* (London: Penguin Books, 2010).
3. Carol S. Dweck, *Mindset* (New York: Ballantine Books, 2017).
4. Dweck, *Mindset*.
5. Simon Sinek, David Mead, and Peter Docker, *Find Your Why: A Practical Leadership Book to Bring Purpose to Your Team* (London: Penguin Books, 2017).
6. Pauline R. Clance and Suzanne A. Imes, "The Imposter Phenomenon in High Achieving Women: Dynamics and Therapeutic Intervention," *Psychotherapy: Theory, Research & Practice* 15, no. 3 (1978): 241–47. https://doi.org/10.1037/h0086006.
7. Charlotte Hu, "Why Writing by Hand Is Better for Memory and Learning," *Scientific American*, February 21, 2024. https://www.scientificamerican.com/article/why-writing-by-hand-is-better-for-memory-and-learning/.

Chapter 4

1. https://www.independent.ie/tag/gina-london
2. James Clear, *Atomic Habits: An Easy & Proven Way to Build Good Habits & Break Bad Ones* (New York: Avery, 2018).

Chapter 5

1. https://www.julieburstein.com/

Chapter 7

1. Ryan Holiday and Stephen Hanselman, *The Daily Stoic: 366 Meditations on Wisdom, Perseverance, and the Art of Living* (New York: Portfolio, 2016).
2. https://en.wikipedia.org/wiki/Albert_Mehrabian
3. Nick Morgan, "Debunking the Debunkers—The Mehrabian Myth Explained (Correctly)," *Public Words*, July 23, 2009. https://publicwords.com/2009/07/23/debunking-the-debunkers-the-mehrabian-myth-explained-correctly/.
4. Liz Wiseman, *Multipliers, Revised and Updated: How the Best Leaders Make Everyone Smart* (New York: Harper Business, 2017).
5. https://thepincusgroup.com/about-us/meet-our-team/
6. https://jdschramm.com/about/
7. Stuart Diamond, *Getting More: How You Can Negotiate to Succeed in Work and Life* (New York: Crown Business, 2012).

Chapter 8

1. https://www.wendysuzuki.com/
2. https://www.ted.com/talks/amy_cuddy_your_body_language_may_shape_who_you_are
3. https://www.tonyrobbins.com/

Index